Uniform 1794 to 1807

Although little contemporary information on the dress of this period is known to the authors, the plate given in Webster's history, published in 1870, is reproduced here as at least broadly illustrative of the Regiment's appearance at this time (Fig. 1). Mr. Carman has suggested that the probable inspiration for this is a contemporary uncoloured print by Eliot and Taylor. The uniform is described by both Webster and Freeman as being a short scarlet coat with yellow facings and silver buttons placed in twos, with white leather breeches. The helmet was of the bearskin-crested Light Dragoon pattern, with a black cloth turban and silver chain work, and a white over red feather at the left hand side. The waistcoats, gloves and belts, were white. Officers wore a crimson sash over their waistcoats. The horse harness was of brown leather with a white headstall; the bright blue saddle cloth had an edging of a double white line with a white rose in the corner. The cloak cases were white, edged in red, the pistol holsters being covered with bearskin flounces. On field days, the hair was ordered to be dressed and queued and Regimental Orders reminded all ranks that their horses should 'be well trimmed and their tails cut short in the military mode'. The Regiment's motto was to be 'Pro Aris et Focis' (For our Altars and our Hearths) and the county emblem of the Stafford knot was adopted as its badge. The Regiment was armed with pistols and the first issue of swords is described by Freeman as being 'of an old-fashioned make with a black leather scabbard'.

As explained above, little hard information has survived from this period. Paradoxically, however, it must be stated that three pieces of information that have survived appear to challenge certain details of the general description given above.

Firstly, Mr. Carman has brought to our attention a portrait of Sir Nigel Gresley, Bt., showing him wearing the first uniform of the Regiment, but with black facings and black leather belts. This officer served in the Lichfield Troop from the beginning until about 1804, leading one to expect that he would wear the normal Regimental uniform. However, Willson's chart of 1806 is, in fact, the first contemporary confirmation of the Regiment's facing colour as yellow, and Mr. Carman has suggested that perhaps the facing colour was actually black in the beginning, and was changed to yellow in 1799, when the government supplied new clothing, or in 1803, when the Regiment was re-activated on the resumption of war. The fact that the helmet had a black turban at this time may add strength to this theory.

Secondly, a leather crested Light Dragoon pattern helmet of the period was offered for sale in 1988 as an officers helmet of the pattern worn by the Regiment from 1794 to 1801. This had a red, as opposed to black turban, and a plate on the right side bearing a crowned 'GR' cypher and garter over a Stafford knot. On its left side was what was described as a white over red feather 'hackle'. The presence of chin scales on this example suggests that this may have been of the later, slightly larger, type of helmet.

Thirdly, a Hawkes 'Book of Dies' dating from c.1797 to c.1803, preserved in the AMOT collection, shows an interesting helmet plate pattern for the Staffordshire Yeomanry, dated 12 July 1800. Although most of the other patterns recorded in the book are of plates for the 'Tarleton' type of

Fig. 1: Officer, 1794. The anonymous interpretation of the Regiment's first uniform given in Webster's History. *Wolverhampton Public Libraries*

Fig. 2: Simkin's interpretation of an officer and trumpeter in the uniform introduced in 1808. Note that he has given the trumpeter white braid instead of the blue braid indicated by Freeman, and corroborated by Regimental Orders. *Regimental collection*

Fig. 3: (left) Officer and charger, c. 1837. This is thought to be Captain William Mott of the Lichfield Troop. He wears the plain field jacket with white facings and shoulder scales. *AMOT*

Fig. 4: Captain the Hon. W. Bagot's shako, minus its plume. This headdress replaced the 'Tarleton' style Light Dragoon helmet in 1837. *Private collection*

Light Dragoon helmet, the shape of the Staffordshire example is quite different, and is closer to that which would be expected for the Heavy Cavalry, or 'Austrian' type of helmet introduced for regular cavalry in 1812, being quite deep, with the top edge rising to a point in the centre[1]. Unfortunately, no details of the colour of metal used are given. It is felt that this is likely to be a design for the front plate of a trumpeter's or farrier's fur cap, although no other corroborative evidence of its actual introduction into the Regiment has been found.

Although no description of an undress uniform survives, it is clear that the Regiment had one, as reference to the men's 'watering dresses' is made in Regimental orders for February 1804.

A statement of costs of the clothing of the Lichfield Troop for 1803 lists a recruit's jacket as costing £2.12.6, his helmet as £3.3.0, and his cloak as £3.2.0 It also states that each recruit will supply his own boots, breeches and cloak case, and will also be required to bear the cost of having his saddle altered, '....which costs about 3d for each'.

Carbines appear to have been issued about 1800, and a surviving stores inventory taken at Lichfield in February 1801 includes twenty two 'Caribin Bockets and Straps' and twenty three 'Caribin Swivels'. Twelve were distributed to each troop, to men who acted as skirmishers on the flank. Canteens, haversacks and feed bags were issued to at least some of the Regiment, as a Regimental order of 1804 refers to them being required in marching order.

Few dependable details of the dress of the Association and Volunteer troops have been unearthed by the authors. Willson's Volunteer Chart, however, states that a similar uniform of scarlet coat, faced yellow with white breeches was worn by all except the Stone and Eccleshall Troop, which had black facings and gold (or yellow) lace, and the Uttoxeter Troop, which is recorded as having no lace. It must be remembered, however, that this document was not published until 1806 and that the details may not necessarily be appropriate for the earlier period.

Additionally, copies of two intriguing, if naively executed, paintings exist in the AMOT collection, described as relating to one Corbet Howard of the 'Wolverhampton Yeomanry'. Although it is impossible to be sure, it is likely that they may in fact depict a member of the cavalry troop of the Wolverhampton Armed Association. They show a man wearing the crested Light Dragoon ('Tarleton') helmet, a laced Light Dragoon jacket, extending a little below the waist, with narrow metal shoulder chains, white breeches, boots, and a white sword belt. As the photograph is black and white, it is difficult to guess the colours of the original paintings. However, the authors would suggest that the jacket, which has fifteen lines of lace, was blue with a black collar. His helmet has a metal scroll plate above the visor, the first few letters of 'Wolverhampton' being visible upon it.

1. See page 17.

Historical Notes 1808 to 1815

The total strength of the yeomanry and volunteer cavalry of the county in 1808 was recorded as follows:

The Staffordshire Regiment of Yeomanry   400
Loyal Bilston Troop   57
Uttoxeter Troop   57
Stone and Eccleshall Troop   59
Loyal Handsworth Troop   42
Tamworth Troop   48

In 1809, the annual Permanent Duty of thirteen days was held in Derby. Also during the year, a band was established, financed by the officers.

In 1813, new regulations ordered that single troops of volunteer cavalry were either to be amalgamated to form larger units or transferred into existing regiments. The Stone and Eccleshall, the Tamworth and the Uttoxeter Troops all agreed to join the Regiment, leaving the Loyal Handsworth as the only independent troop in the county. However, in the Spring of 1814, peace was declared before these arrangements could be carried out and the Stone and Eccleshall, having agreed to serve only for the duration of the war, requested, and was granted, permission to disband itself. The majority of the Uttoxeter, also being on the same footing, resigned, with the exception of

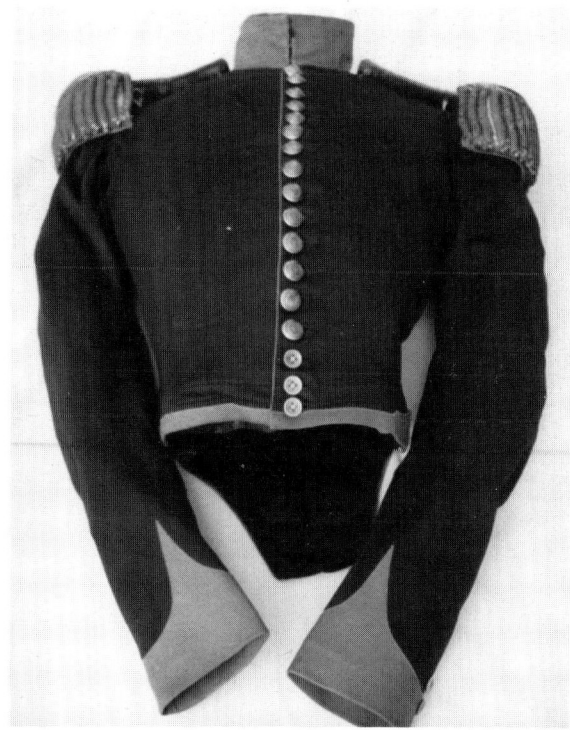
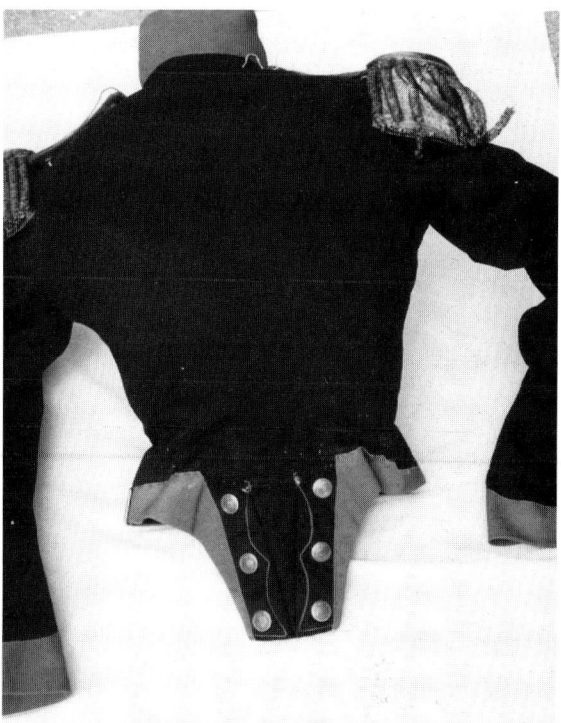
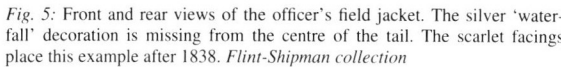

Fig. 5: Front and rear views of the officer's field jacket. The silver 'waterfall' decoration is missing from the centre of the tail. The scarlet facings place this example after 1838. *Flint-Shipman collection*

twenty men under Cornet Wood, who elected to continue, and were attached to the Lichfield Troop. The whole of Tamworth Troop joined the Regiment.

The Regiment now comprised eight troops: the Stafford, Weston, Teddesley, Leek, Walsall, Bilston, Tamworth and the Lichfield – a total of 428 NCOs and men, plus some 30 officers.

In August 1815, in contrast to the work it was usually called upon to perform, the Regiment had the pleasant duty of escorting the Marquess of Anglesey on his public entry into Lichfield after the Waterloo campaign. Similarly, in November of the same year it provided guards and escorts during the visit of the Prince Regent to the Marquess at Beaudesert. This bout of ceremonial was, however, short-lived.

The ending of the wars against Bonaparte seemed to signal the beginning of a period of great unrest in the county – a period in which the Staffordshire Yeomanry would consequently be heavily engaged in assisting the Civil Power. In the half-century preceding Waterloo, events like the American and French Revolutions, together with the gradual propagation of the new populist ideals of liberty and democracy, brought about a desire for change, mainly amongst those enduring hardship at the lower end of society. At the same time, among the propertied classes, these circumstances created a great deal of suspicion and fear of the imminent, and possibly bloody, overthrow of the status quo. Moreover, against this national background, the economic situation in the industrial area of South Staffordshire known as the 'Black Country' had become extremely serious with the ending of the war and the resultant serious stagnation of the iron and coal trades.

On 14 November 1815 the Stafford, Weston and Teddesley troops were ordered to Wolverhampton in response to disturbances which had broken out there. Large numbers of discharged ironworkers and colliers from works in Wolverhampton and Bilston had gathered in Bilston and, although no violence had yet occurred, they were in ugly mood. The arrival of the three troops was greeted with a shower of brickbats. Although the yeomen found it difficult to charge the mob, as a result of the protestors' ability to retreat amongst the coal workings and spoil tips, a few ringleaders were captured. The situation was so serious that the following day the magistrates called out the rest of the Regiment, together with the 9th Light Dragoons and some regular infantry. Peace was restored by the 18th November, however, and the Regiment was dismissed with the thanks of the Lord Lieutenant.

Fig. 6: Another view of the officer's field jacket, showing the silver epaulettes bearing gilt Stafford knots. *Flint-Shipman collection*

Fig. 7: Two slightly different examples of the officer's dress pouch. This general pattern continued in use until 1914.
Regimental collection

Uniform 1808 to 1815

In 1808, the uniform of the Regiment underwent a complete change. For the men, a blue Hussar style jacket with white frogging across the front, white collar and cuffs with three rows of white metal buttons, was taken into wear. The collar, cuffs and back seams were also decorated with white braid. The white leather breeches and black knee boots were still worn but a new, slightly larger, pattern of 'Tarleton' style helmet, albeit with similar appointments to the previous pattern, was introduced. Belts remained white, but blue cloaks with white collars were issued, as was horse furniture in the form of bridle, breast-plate, crupper, pad and bearskin covered holsters. The trumpeters and bandsmen were recorded as receiving white jackets with blue braid. As hardly any contemporary evidence of the details of this uniform survives, we have to assume that officers wore a similar style, with silver lace substituted for the white worsted, but with the buff leather breeches now being augmented by blue pantaloons. Simkin's interpretation of this uniform is given at Fig. 2.

Colonel Monckton's Regimental Orders, given at Somerford on 24 March 1808, announced the changes. Although short on detailed description of the garments themselves, the original text gives us an idea of the administrative and financial considerations involved in such a major change.

'Colonel Monckton having made arrangements for the new clothing of the Regiment begs the attention of the Commanding Officers of Troops to the following details. The uniform to be blue with white facings. The Regiment will be furnished with new jackets, cloaks, helmets and feathers, Bridles, Breast plates, Cruppers and Pads, and such new flounces for the Holsters as may be absolutely wanted. The Serjeants will also be supplied with proper sashes. Cloth and Trimmings for the jackets and Cloaks, with Lace and Buttons, will be sent to the Captains of Troops for their non-commissioned officers and private gentlemen.

The Helmets and feathers will be supplied by Hawkes & Co. Piccadilly, and those now in wear of the Regiment are to be returned to them in the Packages in which the new ones are sent, and the Captains of Troops are requested to send the whole of the Helmets they may have in their possession of the present uniform, keeping an exact account of their number and the condition they are in.

The Captains of Troops may employ whom they think proper to supply the Articles of saddlery according to patterns sent them, and for which the undermentioned allowances will be made.

Regimental Bridle	–/14/6
Breast Plate	–/3/6
Crupper	–/1/8
Large size Pad	–/5/0

The actual expense of fitting up the Flounces

Fig. 8: Officer's black leather undress pouch and belt, *c.* 1840, the pouch bearing the letters 'QORY'. A similar example exists in the Regimental Collection with a reversed 'VR' cypher beneath the crown. *Flint-Shipman collection*

A pattern of jacket and Cloak will be sent to each Troop, and the Captains are desired to pay the most particular attention that no deviation be made therefrom. The Tailors should be instructed to overlay the seam of the jacket so as to admit enlargement or alteration.

Twelve shillings and sixpence will be allowed to the Tailors for making a Jacket and Cloak. But this allowance is not to be paid to them until the Regiment shall have undergone an Inspection by a Field Officer, and a report made by him to the Colonel that the Clothing is well made, and properly fitted and strictly informable to the pattern.

The Trumpeters jackets will be made in London. The Farriers jackets to be the same as the Privates with a Horse shoe of white cloth upon the right arm; and to insure uniformity in this article they will be made by one Tailor and sent to the Captains of Troops.

The allowances specified above will be issued to the Captains as soon as the whole is completed.

Officers

No allowance is made for officer's clothing.

Pattern jackets, Great Coats, Pantaloons, overalls and white dress waistcoats are left for the Inspection of the Officers at Meyer & Magoes (?), No. 25 Mortimer Street, Cavendish Square. Pattern dress swords and Black Belts are to be seen at Hawkes & Co's Piccadilly. The Adjutant has also directions to allow his Regimentals to be inspected by the officers when he receives them from London. It is recommended to the officers to send to Hawkes the measures for their Helmets.

A Medical Staff uniform will shortly be fixed upon for the Regiment and the particulars made known to the Gentlemen of that department.

It will of course be understood that the new Articles of equipment are not to be worn until the whole Regiment is completed.

Fig. 9: Private wearing the newly introduced Light Dragoon tunic of 1859. The first type of 'Albert' helmet with black plume and acorn finial is shown. *Author's collection*

Fig. 11: Officer's forage cap, *c.* 1860. Blue, with silver figuring and edging to peak. Silver lace band with gilt embroidered knot. *Regimental collection*

It is Colonel Monckton's intention to assemble the Regiment for a few days in June, and that the Gentlemen may have the longest possible notice he begs it may notified to them that the meeting will take place between the middle and the end of that month.

By Order of Colonel Monckton,
R. Mayne, Adjt., S.Y.C.

The reference to the gentlemen of the 'Medical Staff' of the Regiment is most intriguing. Unfortunately, no other reference to this department, its uniform or organisation, has been found.

Contemporary descriptions of uniform items are virtually non-existent for this period, but an entry in the Adjutant's Orderly Book for May 1809, listing the 'Orders Of Parade', is worthy of quotation as it lists many items of uniform and accoutrements in use at this time.

Fig. 10: Simkin's impression of a cornet in the 1859 uniform. Although there is no evidence that the regiment actually wore them, he has been depicted wearing the booted overalls fashionable at this time in the Regular Cavalry. *Regimental collection*

Fig. 12: Trumpeter Gladman, about 1860, with one of the 1845 presentation trumpets. Gladman later became bandmaster of the regiment, and went on to obtain the same appointment in the 15th Hussars. *AMOT*

Fig. 13: The officers, from a photograph taken at the Annual Training of May 1861, showing the frock coat and the stable jacket, together with three types of undress headgear. *Regimental collection*

Marching Order. The following articles shall be neatly packed in the cloak case: 3 shirts, 2 pair of stockings, a comb, a clothes brush, 2 shoe brushes, a brush and a piece of sponge for pipe clay, a shaving case, curry comb and brush.

To be folded in the horse cloth and carried over the cloak case: Stable jacket, trowsers, forage cap, a pair of shoes, a snaffle bridle.

A baggage strap to be buckled around the cloak case and the horse cloth, the water deck to be placed over both, and the whole fastened to the saddle with the 2 remaining baggage straps.

In the short holster: a picker, mane comb, and 2 fore horse shoes, and a set of nails. The cloak to be rolled 40 inches long and strapped over the holsters.

The men in Regimental jackets, helmets and feathers cased, white leathern breeches, boots and spurs, white gloves, horse collar, arms and accoutrements.

Watering Order: Stable jacket, trowsers, shoes and forage cap: Horse in snaffle-bridle, and head-collar, horse cloth and surcingle.

Church and Dress Foot Parade: Regimental jacket, helmet and feather uncased, leathern breeches, boots and spurs, sword and belt.

Undress Foot Parade: Stable jacket, trowsers, forage cap and shoes.

All guards will be mounted in full regimentals, boots and spurs, arms and accoutrements.

The manner of turning out for common Field Days and Drills will be specified in the orders of the day.

Officers: On evening foot parade, officers to be in blue pantaloons, hussar boots and spurs, dress swords and black belts, Regimental white waistcoats; the jackets to be worn open and the sashes under them. At all other times they will appear in blue overalls and the jackets closely buttoned. Leather breeches not to be worn, but when orders are particularly given for that purpose.

Orders regarding Church Parade while on permanent duty at Derby in June 1809 refer to dress for this purpose as being:

The men in full Regimental jacket, leathern breeches, boots and spurs, and swords. No Cartridge Belts. The Officers to be dressed in blue pantaloons, Hussar boots and spurs. Jackets buttoned close up and sashes over them. Dress swords and belts. The feathers of the Regimental uncased.

Notwithstanding all the obvious hard work and attention to detail shown by the adjutant, as quoted above, it is interesting to note that, at the inspection of the Regiment made in October 1810 by Lt.-Colonel Corbet, the Inspecting Field Officer, all was by no means well with the appearance of the men on parade. Corbet addressed a scathing report to Colonel Monckton, in which, as well as mentioning '...a great deal of relaxation as to the Yeomen's attendance...', he criticised the poor standard of cleanliness and serviceability of the pistols issued to the men, and the lack of uniformity in the yeomen's appointments. The flurry of regimental orders which inevitably followed has not, unfortunately, survived. However, suffice to say, the tone of the report Corbet made on the following year's inspection was glowing.

Historical Notes 1816 to 1834

A new pattern of carbine was issued to the regiment in 1816, although still at the same level as previously, i.e. twelve per troop.

In March 1817, the Newcastle and Pottery Troop was raised for the Regiment by William Kinnersley, a banker of Newcastle and MP for the Borough.

The deep and general distress amongst the poorer classes of the county seems to have reached such a pitch as the Winter of 1819 approached that it was feared that a general rising would take place in the northern counties. As a consequence of this, a special meeting of the Lieutenancy and Magistracy of the county was held at the Shire Hall in Stafford in November, to discuss the desirability of augmenting the forces of Staffordshire. Although Freeman notes that one result of this was the raising of an infantry force of five companies, no evidence has been uncovered to corroborate this, or the extent to which such a force was attached to the yeomanry. By the end of the year, the Regiment had twelve troops and an establishment of 1,016, including 55 officers.

Actual enrolled strength was 885, including 47 officers, and the troops were as follows:

Troop	Raised	Commander
Stafford and Cheadle	1794	Capt. Lord F. Leveson-Gower
Lichfield	1794	Capt. Sir R. Gresley
Leek	1794	Capt. J. Cruso
Walsall	1794	Capt. J.V. Barber
Weston	1800	Capt. H. Crocket
Teddesley	1803	Capt. E Monckton
Bilston	1805	Capt. W.S. Bickley
Tamworth	1813	Capt. E. Peel
Newcastle and Pottery	1817	Capt. W.S. Kinnersley
Burton	1819	Capt. H. Worthington
Uttoxeter and Blithfield	1819	Capt. W. Bagot
Himley and Enville	1819	Capt. T. Hawkes.

Among the many calls to duty attended to by the Regiment during this period were:

The Leek Troop's part, in March 1817, in breaking up the march of 400 'Blanketeers' from Manchester in their attempt to meet the Prime Minister in London to discuss their grievances. Serious disturbances of colliers and other workers in Wolverhampton and the Black Country of South Staffordshire in April 1822 escalated to such a degree that six troops were involved throughout the month, the Himley in particular having remained out on duty for 23 consecutive days. The staff of the local Militia, the Handsworth Cavalry, as well as several Regular detachments were also involved. In July 1826, the Walsall, the Sandwell (as the Bilston had been renamed) and the Himley were ordered to West Bromwich and Wednesbury to attend to a gathering of colliers protesting against wage cuts. The Himley Troop was badly stoned, but maintained discipline and cleared the area in an orderly fashion. In June 1831, the Burton Troop was called to Tutbury to prevent quell the serious disorder which had broken amongst the population after the discovery of a treasure chest in the River Dove. The Uttoxeter and Burton Troops were called to the serious rioting which had broken out in the neighbouring county town of Derby in October of the same year.

In 1827, the last remaining independent troop in the county, the Loyal Handsworth Volunteer Cavalry, had been disbanded as a result of the new government regulations promulgated in that year. In January 1832, Captain Hordern had obtained permission for the Teddesley Troop to be known henceforth as the Wolverhampton Troop.

It would appear that there were great variations in age among the captains of the troops around this time, as it is recorded that, in April 1832, Captain the Hon. W. Bagot, having come of age, was presented with a silver salver as a testimonial, by his Uttoxeter Troop, the command of which he had succeeded to at the age of 16. Captain Thomas Hawkes, on the other hand, who had raised the Himley Troop in 1819, remained its commanding officer until 1843, when, at the age of 64, he retired in favour of the Hon. Dudley Ward.

Uniform 1816 to *c*.1834

The uniform of the Regiment was changed this year to a pattern similar to that ordered for Regular Light Dragoons in 1811. A blue double-breasted coatee was issued, faced on the collar and cuffs with white and with the back seams outlined with white; white metal buttons and shoulder scales (epaulettes for officers) were worn. Freeman's notes indicate that new 'blue-green' overalls with double white stripes replaced the buff leather breeches. Webster's history, however, describes the new netherwear as 'Wellington trousers' of grey cloth. The old bearskin-crested Light Cavalry helmets were still worn, with a soft muffin-shaped round forage cap with white band and button, for undress. Belts were still of white leather with black pouches. Sheepskins, valises and new saddlery were also issued. Also this year, at the request of the Colonel, the Heavy Dragoon pattern of carbine was supplied to the Regiment. However, these were soon replaced by the Light Dragoon pattern – although, again, only on a basis of 12 per troop.

Once again, no contemporary illustration of this uniform is known to the authors, and, in our opinion, a questionable interpretation by Simkin, depicting an almost completely 'regulation' regular Light Dragoon kit for this period, including sabretache, shabrack, etc., has to be doubted as a dependable reference, mainly as the result of his inclusion of a shako, which was not adopted until 1837.

The only other reference to be found concerning uniform at this period arises in October 1816, when Captain Terry and the Walsall Troop were called upon to quell riots which had broken out in the town. We are told that, as the troop had not yet completed the process of taking into use the new uniform, it was unable to turn out.

Historical Notes 1835 to 1859

In October 1835, the Regiment was presented with five squadron standards, described by Freeman as, '...of the most elaborate and costly description...' That of the 1st Squadron was crimson, emblazoned with '...the well-known badges of England...', and the other four were of white silk, bearing the Stafford knot in the centre, enclosed by a garter with the regimental motto and a wreath surmounted by the Royal Crown. With each standard was presented '...a superbly laced standard belt', two of which, together with two of the standards, are preserved in the Regimental collection. The coronation of Queen Victoria took place in June 1838 and, in commemoration of the

Fig. 15: Officer's 'Albert' helmet, of the type introduced in 1850, but with the later white plume with flat rosette top. *Regimental collection*

Fig. 14: Watercolour, after P. W. Reynolds, of Cornet the Hon. Henry Ryder of the Stafford Troop, in stable dress, 1861.

Fig. 16: Trumpeter John Brown, a Light Brigade veteran of the 17th Lancers, wearing the 'kepi' style forage cap, *c.* 1870. *Private collection*

escorts provided by the Regiment on her visit to Shugborough six years previously, one of her first acts was to bestow the honour of a Royal title upon the Regiment, which became known as The Queen's Own Royal Regiment of Staffordshire Yeomanry Cavalry.

The Regiment was used for extended periods during the Chartist troubles from 1839 to 1842, when the Potteries experienced serious disturbances. On one occasion, at Lane End (or Longton), where barricades had been erected in the streets, the Newcastle Troop had been ordered to open fire upon the mob and one man was seriously wounded. The scale of these disturbances is indicated by the fact that the number of defendants in the subsequent trials totalled 274, of whom 165 were goaled, and 54 were transported, 11 for life. In July 1839, serious rioting had broken out following a large Chartist meeting in Brimingham. As a consequence, several troops of the Staffordshire, together with some of the Worcestershire, were placed on duty in the area, at Himley and Handsworth, patrolling the roads and keeping watch for a period of ten days.

In 1840, Lord Paget, who had recently become captain of the Burton Troop, obtained permission for it to be henceforth called the Anglesey Troop. In October 1841, a committee was set up to raise funds for the purchase of a lasting testimonial to the Regiment in recognition of the services it had rendered during the preceeding long period of disturbances in the county. Similarly, the value of the Regiment was recognised by a number of the influential inhabitants of the Moorlands district in the North East of the county, and it was decided to establish a troop. Both the enthusiasm and the subscription raised exceeded expectations, and a squadron, to be known as the Moorlands Squadron, its troops based in Cheadle and Leek, was established in December 1842. In June 1843, a halt was made at Uttoxeter on their way to the Annual Training at Lichfield, and the squadron was presented with a standard by the Earl of Shrewsbury on behalf of his wife, whose gift it was. Although the facing colour had been changed since standards had last been presented, Freeman notes that Moorlands' standard was similar in all respects to those already in use by the Regiment. At the Training itself, the Regiment marched in over 700 strong, out of an enrolled strength of 786. In 1845, the Regiment was presented with twelve silver trumpets, purchased by the subscription set up in 1841. These still exist in the Regimental collection, and one is shown being held by Trumpeter Gladman in Fig. 12.

Among other details, Sleigh's *The Royal Militia And Yeomanry Cavalry Army List* of 1850 quotes for the Regiment the highest Effective Strength of all those recorded:

'1 Lieut.-Col. Commandant, 1 Lieut.-Colonel, 2 Majors, 11 Captains, 22 Lieutenants, 11 Cornets, 1 Adjutant, 1 Surgeon, 1 Assist.-Surgeon, 1 Vety.-Surgeon, 1 Regimental Serjt.-Major, 11 Troop Quartermasters, 11 Troop Sergt.-Majors, 33 Sergeants, 44 Corporals, 11 Trumpeters, 11 Farriers, 770 Privates. Total Non-Com. Officers and Privates, 892. The Regiment is composed of 11 Troops, forming 6 Squadrons.'

Uniform *c.* 1834 to 1859

Freeman's notes for 1834 state, rather cryptically, 'About this time some slight alterations were made in the uniform of the regiment, a new pattern shoulder scale being introduced, by which a great difference was effected.' In fact, evidence from Regimental Orders suggests that quite a significant alteration was made, involving the changing of the double breasted Light Dragoon coatee for a single breasted version. A note in AMOT files describes a coatee of Lieutenant T.B. Chinn, of the Lichfield Troop, from this period. The blue jacket has white collar and cuffs, silver lace on collar and cuffs, narrow white piping down front. Light Dragoon skirts, with white turnbacks. Fourteen silver half-ball buttons with plain Stafford knot. The silver epaulettes would have borne gilt Stafford knots. The fine braiding within the laced edges of the collar is formed into small Stafford knots. The dress trousers are blue, with a silver oak lace stripe, full scallop, about 2 or 2¼in. wide.

In addition, a portrait of about 1837, thought to be of Captain Mott of the Lichfield Troop, reveals the existence of a much plainer garment, of the type which a later reference[2] describes as the 'Field Jacket' (see Fig. 3). It is blue,

2. See page 17.

Fig. 17: Lt. Cathcart Boycott Wight of the Himley Troop, *c.* 1871. Note the dress overalls with silver lace stripes, and that the helmet plume has changed to white by this date. *Collection of R. G. Harris*

Fig. 18: Dress sabretache. This general pattern appears to have remained unchanged throughout the period when sabretaches were worn. *Regimental collection*

single breasted, with approximately 20 buttons, with plain white collar and pointed cuffs, and is worn with shoulder scales.

Reference to the Regimental Orderly Book for December 1834 shows that the men's former double breasted garment was altered, presumably in the interests of economy, to make a single breasted undress stable jacket by the removal of the tails and fly, and with the addition of shoulder cords made from the lace removed from the back seams. Although the white coatees of the bandsmen and trumpeters were to be altered in the same way, the blue braid on the back seams was to remain, and extra blue braid was supplied from which to make their shoulder cords.

The position with regard to undress jackets for both officers and men is clarified by reference to the same order when it says: 'Officers when in *undress* will wear a jacket *exactly* similar to that of the men with the exception of their having a silver lace loop on each shoulder, instead of that worn by the men.' The illustration of Lt. the Hon. Henry Ryder (Fig. 14) shows this item still in use in 1861.

Thus, at this time, it would appear that the Regiment went into a hybrid version of the current Regular Light Dragoon coatee, and, moreover, that officers had a much plainer 'Field Jacket', as well as the usual undress item of a stable jacket.

The following order of dress was stipulated in September 1837 for officers at morning parade and in mess:

> '...regimental jacket and scales, darker blue trousers with silver lace, gold laced girdle, sword and sabretache, the silver laced forage cap to be worn at morning parades, except by those officers of duty, who will appear in full uniform, the same as the Picquet Guard. Officers when in the town (presumably at the Annual Training) of a morning will wear undress jackets, blue trousers with the white cloth seams and forage caps with silver lace.'

In 1837, the crested Light Dragoon helmet was at last done away with, the Regiment being one of the last, if not the last, to wear this outdated headgear. It was replaced by a shako with silver ornaments, with white horsehair plume and white cap lines for the men, and white cock feather plume and silver lines for the officers. The chin scales were ordered to be looped up when dismounted. Lord Bagot's shako is depicted in Fig.4. The badge consisted of a gilt crown mounted on a black cockade, above a silver 'Maltese Cross' with a rope edged gilt disc in the centre bearing a silver Stafford knot. An early photograph of a collection of Staffordshire military headdresses shows that a later type of shako, of the more cylindrical pattern ordered for regular Light Dragoons in 1844, was later worn by the Regiment.

An extract from some regimental regulations of this period give details of orders of dress as follows:

1. Marching Order: The valise packed according to order. All the appointments complete. The chacoe covered and without the plume. White gloves.
2. Review Order: All the appointments complete. Chacoe uncovered, and the plume to be worn. Officers with white headcollar, fastened to the off side. White gloves.
3. Drill Order: Stable jacket and forage cap. Blue trowsers. Boots and spurs. Stripped saddles with cloak in front, pouch and belts. Sword and belts. White gloves.
4. Watering Order: Stable jacket and forage cap. White trowsers. Shoes and brass clasps. No belts. Sircingle and blue cloth. Head collar and bridoon.
5. Dress Foot Parade: Dress jacket. Blue trowsers. Chacoe uncovered and plume. Boots and spurs. Sword and belt. White gloves. No pouch or belts to be worn.

Fig. 19: Four men of the Himley Troop, taken at the 1885 Annual Training, showing the boots and pantaloons introduced in 1872, and the 1881 tunic. *Regimental collection*

Fig. 20: Rear view of the other ranks' 1881 tunic. *Regimental collection*

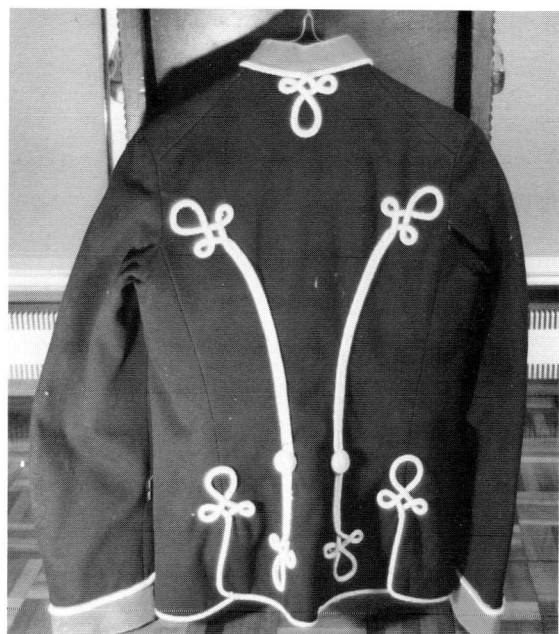

6. Undress Foot Parade: Stable jacket. White trowsers and forage cap. Shoes and brass clasps.
7. Church Parade: Same as Dress Foot Parade.
8. Stable Dress: Same as undress Foot Parade.
9. Guards: Dress jacket. Blue trowsers. Chacoe uncovered and plume. Boots and spurs. Pouch and belts. Sword and belt. White gloves.
Officers Mess Dress: Jacket with scales, gold laced girdle. Dark blue trowsers and silver lace. Boots and spurs, brass. Sword and belt and sabretash.
The above dress will be worn by officers on all evening foot parades with the blue and silver forage cap.

Officers Ball Dress: Full dress jackets, with bullion epaulettes. Dark blue trowsers with silver lace. Boots and spurs, brass. Gold laced girdle. Sword and silver laced belt and pouch, with silver belt. Sabretash of silver, and blue velvet mountings.'

In 1838, as a result of the 'Royal' title having been bestowed upon the Regiment, facings were changed to scarlet. A Regimental order referring to this very significant change is dated 16 July 1838:

'Consequent on the change in title – changes in dress:
Facings and turnbacks of jackets changed to scarlet, buttons bearing the appellation of the regiment will be supplied for the jacket. The last served out blue trousers will have a scarlet stripe substituted for the present white one.
Cloth for the trousers of a dark oxford mixture will be issued out, which will have a double stripe of scarlet on each leg, as worn by Light Dragoons. The forage cap will have a scarlet band and button. Patterns of all the above have been sent to each troop, items should be introduced before next September's Permanent Duty.
Chacoes will be issued to the whole regiment at Lichfield on Permanent Duty, except the Newcastle Troop, who received their supply last September. Officers are referred to Hawkes & Moseley of Piccadilly, for their chacoes.'

Another change involved the shako badge receiving a new centre, with a smaller knot being encircled by a pierced strap bearing the title 'The Queen's Own Royal Yeomanry' within the rope edged disc.

Although some type of officers' decorated pouch and sabretache may well have been worn for some years, it is only around this period that definite evidence of them first appears. A Hawkes' pattern book shows the dimension of the pouch to be 6½ deep by 7¾ long, but their size seems to have diminished over the years. The main features of the decoration on the flap, however, appeared to have changed only in small details. The blue velvet ground is edged with silver lace, and a silver Stafford knot, with fringed ends, is surmounted by a large and fully embroidered Royal crown. The pouch belt was of silver oak lace on red morocco with silver chased buckle, tip and slide. Unusually for a yeomanry regiment, the pickers and chain were gilt. The sabretache had a similar large Royal crown above a large silver knot, on a blue velvet ground, edged with 2 inch silver lace (see Figs. 7 and 18). It is interesting to note that a device consisting of the large Royal (or Queen Victoria's) crown and the knot survived in this Regiment to be worn by other ranks as a cap badge right up to the Second World War and beyond, long after Victoria's had been replaced by the later forms of crown in the badges of the rest of the army.

A similar uncertainty applies to the dates of the introduction of use of undress versions of the pouch and sabretache. Mr. Carman describes an example of a Victorian period undress sabretache, presumably of black leather, as follows:

'...had three separate mounts – a smallish crown over a medium-to-thin Stafford knot with two widespread branches of laurel leaves tied in the middle by a ribbon, metal not known, perhaps white-metal or silver.'[3]

Photographs of an undress black leather pouch and pouch belt, preserved in the Flint-Shipman Collection are given at Fig.8. A similar set is in the Regimental collection, the pouch of which bears instead an intertwined and reversed 'VR' cypher below the crown.

3. See page 17.

Fig. 21: Lt. the Earl of Shrewsbury, wearing the officer's version of the 1881 uniform, c. 1885. *Collection of R. G. Harris*

Fig. 22: Captain Edmund Davenport wears the silver laced stable jacket which replaced the earlier plain version about 1875. *Regimental collection*

Three patterns of trousers are mentioned in Regimental Orders of 1839/40 as being worn by other ranks. White trousers were ordered for stable dress, light blue in drill order, and the 'new' oxford mixture for dress. The Leek and Cheadle troops, however, had still not received their dress trousers by April 1843, and so were to, '...wear their blue trousers on all occasions, except stable dress, when they will wear their white duck ones.'

In 1843, Colonel Monckton requested the officers to '...provide themselves with blue trousers of the same colour and shade as lately served out to the men. They are to have a double stripe of scarlet, each stripe being one inch in width and one eighth of an inch between...'

The correspondence of John Cattlow, a solicitor of Cheadle who was involved in the raising of the Moorlands Squadron in 1842, reveals some interesting details about the early life of the squadron, and gives a list of the arms and accoutrements sent from London in February 1843:

'Carbines, Short Cavalry	12
Pistols, 9 in. C13 with Swivel Ramrods	80
Swords, Light Cavalry Pattern 1822	80
Scabbards, Iron, for ditto	80
Belts, Sword, Waist, complete	80
Knots, Sword	80
Cases	6'

The purpose of the 'Cases' is, unfortunately, not clear. An interesting sidelight on the manner in which some changes in uniform were arranged is hinted at elsewhere in Cattlow's papers. He had, in 1844, become quartermaster of the Cheadle Troop and a letter to him from Edward Heaton, his counterpart of the Leek Troop, says:

'My object in writing to you is to inform you when last at Lichfield the propriety of the quartermasters wearing black belts instead of "Pipe Clays" was discussed at a full meeting of that hon'ble body, when it was unanimously resolved that a deputation should wait upon Col. Monckton to request that he would allow them to do so in future... Quartermaster Shubotham of the Newcastle Troop... has got a complete set from Purdom of Lichfield and recommends that I should do the same.' He had, '...no fear of other objections being raised to our wearing them.' He went on to urge Cattlow not to be, '...behind in his movement,' adding, ' ...of course, I expect the cost to be defrayed out of regimental funds.'

Although we know that the 'Pipe Clays' of the troopers were to be changed some nine years later, we are not told how successful the representations of the quartermasters were on this occasion. What is clear, however, is that, although not commissioned, 'that hon'ble body' were, nevertheless, on account of their important function, men of some influence in the regiment – and were not afraid to advance their cause, at least in matters sartorial.

The pistol was still the only firearm used by the majority of Staffordshire Yeomen, with the exception of the 12 skirmishers per troop, who were issued with carbines. In 1845, however, the first universal issue of carbines took place and instructions were given that every trooper should arrange to have his saddle properly fitted to carry them. This presumably refers to the fitting on the offside of the saddle arch of the small leather 'boot', into which was placed the muzzle of the weapon. No details survive to tell us if new combined pouch and carbine belts were supplied, or if the existing ones were altered.

A surviving tailor's book of about 1848, now held in the National Army Museum, shows an officer's dress jacket of

Fig. 23: A private, about 1890, wearing a version of the 1881 tunic with square-cut skirts. *Author's collection*

blue with scarlet facings, laced similarly to the first single breasted type described above, but with eighteen plain silver buttons, a fixed gold and crimson striped girdle and silver epaulettes. The skirts are still of the regular Light Dragoon style, bearing three-button silver piped flaps and silver 'waterfall' decoration. The ornate cuff decoration consists of a thick silver lace edging to the pointed scarlet cuff with narrower tracing braid forming an inverted Stafford knot at the apex. Above and around the knot is a large and finely traced fern-like decoration. A similar decoration, traced with small Stafford knots, follows the back seams.

In addition to showing the expected form of simple blue, scarlet-faced undress stable jacket (having twenty two buttons), the same book also shows a scarlet faced version of the plain jacket worn by Captain Mott in the portrait of 1837. The pattern is entitled 'Field Jacket' and has sixteen buttons, shoulder scales, and, on the back seams, has a silver cord tracing decoration, surmounted with a trefoil knot, which is much more simplified than that on the dress version. The Light Dragoon skirts, with flap and 'waterfall' are retained. The collar, turnbacks and piping are scarlet.

Although, as is described above, an officer's dress jacket was prescribed, two items of pictorial evidence suggest that the field jacket was also being worn as a dress uniform, at least by the 1850s.

A painting by Selous depicting the various personalities attending the opening of the Great Exhibition in 1851 includes a figure of Earl Granville, a Royal Commissioner, in the uniform of the Regiment. He wears the jacket with silver epaulettes, silver lace pouch belt with fully decorated pouch, and grey overalls with a single silver lace stripe. A watercolour painting by Norie (see back cover), held in the Regimental collection, and depicting seven mounted officers of the Regiment, shows them also wearing this jacket, in this case without the back seam decoration, but with full silver epaulettes, the crimson and gold girdle, and silver lace pouch belt with gilt chains and pickers. The 'Albert' helmet, introduced in 1850 is worn, together with blue overalls with double scarlet stripe. Swords and embroidered sabretache with black leather slings, complete the outfit of most of the figures. A surviving example of the Field Jacket from this period is preserved in the Flint-Shipman collection at Aldershot, and is shown at Figs.5 and 6. The horse furniture depicted in the painting shows brown bridles, cross face pieces with gilt bosses, and black sheepskins with red cloth scalloped edges.

A black 'Albert' pattern helmet, which was to serve, with only a few small alterations, as the Regiments's full dress headgear for forty three years, replaced the shako in 1850. The silver plate is an impressive affair, surmounted by a large crown, and has a gilt Stafford knot encircled by a gilt pierced strap bearing the title 'THE QUEEN'S OWN ROYAL YEOMANRY' on a rayed star, placed upon a plaque, the whole surrounded by a wreath composed of laurel leaves on the left, and oak leaves on the right. The peak has a silver plated binding and is decorated with acanthus leaves. The black horsehair plume issues from an acanthus holder, and is surmounted by an acorn decoration. The first officers' helmets were of leather, but subsequent examples were of japanned metal, as were those of the men. The helmet plates of the men were all white metal (see Fig.15).

The first illustration to be found of an undress uniform for officers relates to this period. Norie's painting, referred to above, shows a partly obscured officer wearing a plain single breasted blue frock coat with no decoration, fastened with silver buttons. No belt is visible, and a soft blue forage cap with a silver lace band and black drooping peak is worn.

Sleigh's List of 1850 gives the following details of the Regiment's dress:

> 'Regimental Appointments: Equipped as Light Dragoons; clothing blue, facings red; lace silver; armed with swords and percussion carbines.
> Officers' uniform: Black helmet with silver ornaments and black plume; Light Dragoon jacket with silver shoulder scales and gold girdle; blue trowsers with scarlet stripes; belts, black with silver mountings. Horse Appointments: Black with black sheepskin.
> Men's uniform: Black helmet etc., with black plume; Light Dragoon jacket with silver scales, blue and white girdle; blue trowsers with scarlet stripes; buff belts. Horse Appointments: brown with black sheepskin.
> Standards: 1st or Royal Standard, crimson and gold, with Royal Arms and designation, "The Queen's Own Royal Yeomanry". 2nd, 3rd, 4th, 5th and 6th Standards, white and gold with crown and Staffordshire knot on silver ground, surrounded with a garter, bearing the motto, "Pro Aris et Focis".'

In 1853, the white buff pouch and sword belts of the men were changed for black leather pouch belts and brown leather sword belts. Photographic evidence suggests that these distinctive items remained the same for the remainder of our period. Freeman, although giving no description,

Fig. 25: Officer's mess kit, c. 1890. The decoration on the vest was removed after 1894. *Regimental collection*

Fig. 24: Troop Quartermaster Horne of the Himley Troop, abut 1890. His 1881 pattern tunic is decorated with silver lace in place of the white braid of other ranks, has silver shoulder cords, and silver lace edging around the top of the collar. He wears a sabretache which appears to be plain black leather. Although somewhat hidden by its plume, his helmet is of the usual pattern. *Regimental collection*

Fig. 26: A private of the Wolverhampton Troop in drill order about 1890, wearing the blue stable jacket with scarlet shoulder cords, collar, and pointed cuffs. *Author's collection*

also notes that the old straight spur was replaced by 'one of a more serviceable pattern.'

An undress cap, in the style of the French 'kepi', seems to have made its appearance in the 1850s. Notes from a Hawkes' pattern book of *c.*1857 describe it as being of scarlet cloth, plain peak, silver Stafford Knot, blue welt around the top and up the back, with a 1¾ in. blue band around the base. From pictorial evidence, it appears to have been worn by both officers and men (see especially Figs. 13 & 16).

Historical Notes 1859 to 1880

It may be considered as a sign of the times, particularly in relation to the rise of the Volunteer movement that, in 1861, a Regimental competition was held for musketry in place of that normally held for swordsmanship. In 1865, after serving in the Regiment for 27 years, Captain and Adjutant Davis retired, to be replaced by Captain Webster, who had served in the Mutiny with the 8th Hussars. It was Captain Webster who was to publish his history of the Regiment in 1870. In November 1866, Queen Victoria made her first official visit since the death of the Prince Consort in 1861, to Wolverhampton. Two squadrons, under Major Thorneycroft and Captain Webster, and made up of the Wolverhampton, Walsall, Himley and Lichfield Troops, escorted the royal carriage on this occasion.

The last occasion the Regiment was to be called out on public order duty was to be on 22 February 1867, when the Wolverhampton Troop, under Captain Perry, was called upon to patrol the streets of that town in anticipation of riots against the anti-Roman Catholic activist Murphy, who was speaking there. In the event, there was no disorder and the troop was dismissed the following day.

480 percussion Westley Richards carbines were released to the Regiment from the Military Store Office at Weedon in April 1870, and these were issued to the yeomen during the course of the following year.

With a 'paper' strength of 892 at this time, the Regiment continued to be one of the strongest recruited yeomanry regiments and it was with some dismay that new regulations limiting the number of squadrons allowed in regiments of the yeomanry were received in April 1870. By the following year's training however, relief was felt with the news that special dispensation had been received for the Regiment to retain its twelve troops. The number of officers allowed was, however, reduced to two lieutenants and one cornet per squadron instead of per troop. The establishment of officers was henceforth to be one lieutenant-colonel commandant, one lieutenant-colonel, two majors, twelve captains, twelve lieutenants, five cornets, one adjutant, two surgeons, and one veterinary surgeon, making a total of thirty eight, instead of fifty two commissioned officers. It is of some incidental interest to note that the veterinary surgeon at this time had faithfully served the Regiment in the same capacity since 1816!

The new regulations also laid down an establishment for each troop of: one Quartermaster, one Troop Serjeant-Major, two Serjeants, two Corporals, and forty Privates. This notwithstanding, the return of troops (excluding officers) attending for duty in 1871 was as follows: Lichfield 55, Stafford 39, Wolverhampton 48, Walsall 48, Tamworth 36, Newcastle squadron (2

Fig. 27: This F. G. O. Stuart photograph shows a serjeant in a frock decorated, at the cuff and around the base of the collar, with silver lace. Although he appears to be a staff-serjeant, he wears the type of forage cap normally associated with the rank of serjeant.
Collection of R. G. Harris

Fig. 28: Most of these men of the Lichfield Troop, *c.* 1892, wear the blue undress frock. The frocks of the staff-serjeants in this group wear a different style of embellishment to that shown in Fig. 27. *Regimental collection*

13

troops) 93, Anglesey 39, Uttoxeter 45, Himley 46, Leek 48, and Cheadle 41, giving a total of 583, out of a total of effectives of 650. The year 1872, however, was to see a considerable falling off of membership on account not only of the new regulations, but also of the shortage of mounts brought about by the demand caused by the Franco-Prussian War.

Freeman notes that new drill regulations introduced at the 1876 Training did away with the use of the regimental guidons, and they were not carried at the inspection parade. Following the death of Captain Webster in 1877, Captain the Hon. Heneage Legge, 9th Lancers, succeeded as Adjutant, being the first of the adjutants seconded to the Regiment for the purpose from their Regular regiments. At the Annual Training at Lichfield in May 1880, 418 out of the 447 enrolled other ranks attended.

Uniform 1859 to 1880

In 1859 the old coatee uniform was finally discontinued, and a new tunic following the pattern introduced four years previously for regular Light Dragoons, was introduced.

For the men, it was dark blue with scarlet collar and cuffs, the collar having white worsted braid all around, with Austrian knots on the cuffs and white shoulder cords. Across the breast were five white cord loops with caps and drops. The white piping extended down both leading edges, and around the skirts. This is seen in Fig.9. For officers, the tunic was fastened by silver toggles, was edged all round with silver cord, and had five rows of silver cords, caps and drops. The back seams were traced with the same braid, with caps at waist level, forming a trefoil knot at the top, and an Austrian knot at the bottom. Examination of a surviving example shows the rows gradually diminishing in length from 7 inches at the top of each side to 4 inches at the bottom. Rank was indicated by the system of gilt crown and star introduced in the Regular Army in 1855. These were placed upon the collar, which was decorated by the addition of single 3/4 inch silver lace along the top for junior officers, and a further line of the same around the bottom for field officers. Rank was indicated on the cuff for junior officers in the form of a system, similar to that of the 6th Dragoon Guards, of silver 'wheels' in tracing braid surrounding the knot. For field officers, cuffs were decorated in the Royal Artillery style, with complex tracing surrounding a lace chevron. In April 1868 a double stripe of silver lace was approved for officers' full dress overalls.

At the same time as the introduction of the new tunic, the plume on the helmet was ordered to be changed to one of white horsehair. Photographic evidence suggests that this change did not take place, however, and the black plume continued to be worn, at least until about 1870 (See Figs.9,10 and 12). A contemporary account describes the plume as still being worn in the straggling style depicted in the earlier Norie watercolour.

Orders issued on the occasion of the Royal visit to Wolverhampton in 1866 instruct that:

> 'Every member will see that all his appointments are well cleaned and all buckles, chains, bits, stirrup irons, &c., polished and the horses heels trimmed.
> REVIEW ORDER
> Tunic, double striped overalls, helmet, pouch belt and carbine, sword and belt, cloak, valise and sheepskin.'

Undress uniform for the men at this time was the blue stable jacket with scarlet collar and scarlet pointed cuffs, edged down the front with scarlet piping. Shoulder cords were of twisted worsted, also scarlet. This was worn with the 'kepi' forage cap. Officers still wore a similar garment, of the type originally described above for 1834, which had more buttons than the mens', and silver lace shoulder cords. Also worn by officers was a blue frock coat of the

Fig. 29: Serjeant Cork of the Lichfield Troop. He displays an impressive 'armful' of proficiency badges, together with four 'Dartmouth', or long service badges, indicating at least 15 years service. *Regimental collection*

Fig. 30: This corporal of the Wolverhampton Troop wears the distinctively decorated forage cap peculiar to this rank. *Regimental collection*

contemporary Regular cavalry style, decorated across the breast with six lines of black braid, fastened with olivets, and each line having an olivet placed at either end. Austrian knots in black braid decorated the cuffs. The officers' group of 1861, shown at Fig.13, shows both these garments being worn with three different types of undress headgear: the blue peaked forage cap with horizontal silver edged peak and gilt knot on silver lace band, an extant example of which is shown at Fig.11; a similar item apparently updated simply by the removal of the peak; and the 'kepi' described above.

In May 1871, Lt. Col. Lord Bagot wrote to all the officers asking their opinion on the possible introduction of 'Napoleon' boots and pantaloons being introduced for the men. He believed that they would be a more practical dress in view of the heavy wear and tear overalls were subject to, and added, by way of support for his idea, the information that the Gloucestershire Hussars and Huntingdonshire Light Horse Volunteers were 'much satisfied with them'. The response in favour of some type of high boot was presumably positive and, in February 1872, orders were given for the men to equip themselves with high boots at their own expense, and instructions were given for the single striped overalls to be converted to pantaloons. Both items are to be seen worn by the men in Fig. 19. It will be noticed, however, that what ultimately appeared were, in fact, knee boots, and not the much higher Napoleons originally favoured by his lordship.

Historical Notes 1881 to 1893

At the 1881 Annual Training, 437, including 18 bandsmen, of an enrolled strength of 466, were recorded as present. Snider carbines were issued this year, and a cup was given by the officers for an annual shooting competition. In 1882, due to a falling off in numbers, the Tamworth Troop was struck off the roll. At this year's Annual Training, the Regiment, together with several local Volunteer and Militia units, were inspected by Field Marshal HRH The Duke of Cambridge. The Duke expressed pleasant surprise at how well the horses appeared on parade, remarking '...that it was a very creditable and fine turn-out.' The 1883 Training saw no less than 107 recruits in the ranks, with the Regiment as a whole marching in 474 strong, of an enrolled strength of 495. Following the death of Colonel W. Bromley-Davenport during the 1884 Training, Major and Hon. Lt.-Colonel the Marquis of Anglesey was promoted to the command. Martini-Henry carbines were issued to the Regiment in 1885. In 1887, Captain G.F. Talbot was gazetted Major. He had obtained the captaincy of the Stafford Troop in 1872, on his return to England after service in the Prussian 2nd Dragoon Guards in the Franco-Prussian War. The Leek Troop was disbanded in 1889, thus reducing the Regiment to 10 troops of 541 officers and men. Freeman's notes indicate that present at the Training this year were, in addition to the Regiment's 'splendid band', its ambulance and signalling sections.

The Cheadle Troop was disbanded in 1892, the new establishment being fixed at 488 of all ranks in nine troops as follows: A – Lichfield, B – Stafford, C – Wolverhampton, D – Walsall, E – 1st Newcastle, F – 2nd Newcastle, G – Anglesey, H – Uttoxeter, and I – Himley. In March 1892, a detachment took part in manoeuvres with some 14th Hussars and the Regular troops then stationed at Whittington Barracks. The yeomanry detachment acquitted itself well, being instrumental in 'capturing' a party of hussars.

In the Yeomanry reorganisation of 1893, the Staffordshire Yeomanry was brigaded with the Warwickshire Yeomanry to form the 8th Yeomanry Brigade of the 4th Division of the Auxiliary Cavalry. The squadron organisation was introduced and one adjutant was allowed per brigade rather than for each regiment. One permanent serjeant-major was allowed per squadron, instead of per troop, and an additional permanent serjeant-major was allocated to act as regimental serjeant-major. The two Newcastle troops were merged into one, and four squadrons were formed as follows: A – Lichfield and Walsall Troops, B – Newcastle and Stafford Troops, C – Anglesey and Uttoxeter Troops, and D – Himley and Wolverhampton Troops. Although the actual strength of the Regiment at the 1893 Training had fallen to 332, the new establishment was 431, including the brigade adjutant and 25 officers.

Uniform 1881 to 1893

In 1881, the men's Light Dragoon tunic was changed in favour of one which was based on the Hussar style, with six cord loops across the front. The scarlet collar and cuffs were retained, but the white worsted braid now extended around the base of the collar only, forming a trefoil decoration below the back of the collar. The braid continued down the front, around the skirts, extending up each of the two side vents at the rear, and formed similar knots at the top of each one. The same braid formed a trefoil knot at the cuff in place of the former Austrian knot. The back seams were traced with double braid, with trefoil knots at top and bottom, and caps placed on each at the waist. No shoulder cords were fitted, and the skirts of the new garment were worn shorter and were cut away at the front. An intriguing exception to this is shown at Fig.23. Here, a member of what is probably the Newcastle Squadron wears this pattern of tunic, but with square-cut skirts. As is to be expected, the change-over took time and, in March 1882, Troop Serjeant-Majors were ordered to supply the measurements of yeomen to whom the new pattern tunic had not yet been issued. The old tunics were to be kept, however, for drills and on the march.

Fig. 31: Captain Hugh Charrington *c.* 1896. Levee Order. Captain Charrington appears in Levee Order, featuring tight, special pantaloons, together with the Hessian boots which were reserved for this purpose. Also note the newly introduced busby.
Author's collection

15

Fig. 32: Quartermaster Tudor, 'D' or Himley and Wolverhampton Squadron, c. 1895. Quartermaster Tudor wears the newly-issued O.R. pattern busby. He is distinguished as a Warrant Officer by the silver lace on his collar and the silver cord braiding throughout his tunic, which is of the 1881 pattern. His sword appears to be of the 1853 O.Rs' cavalry pattern, probably with a silver knot. *Collection of C. Stewart.*

Fig. 33: Regimental Serjeant Major Brown, c. 1894-5. The Serjeant Major is in Mounted Review Order, as worn from the introduction of the busby until c. 1902-3. His tunic is of the 1881 O.Rs' pattern, but with silver cord, etc. In the horse kit there is a black sheepskin and headchain, while his sword, although carried on the saddle, has the old pattern scabbard and the sword itself appears to be the 1821 O.Rs' Light Cavalry pattern. *Regimental collection*

N.B. The ancient Warrant Rank of Troop or Squadron Quartermaster, long abandoned in the regulars, continued for many years in some yeomanry corps. By the 1890s, however, their numbers had dwindled to a handful. It would appear that Staffordshire was one of the last to abolish this appointment.

The photograph of Lieutenant The Earl of Shrewsbury (Fig.21) shows the officers' version of this tunic, and a Hawkes pattern book for 1883 describes the new tunic for officers as being blue with scarlet facings, trimmed with silver Staff cord, with caps and olivets. The collar lace would be of 6th Dragoon Guards pattern, and the silver cord Austrian knots on the sleeve were traced both sides with silver Russia braid. The cuffs of Field Officers continued to be laced in the style of the Royal Artillery.

Regimental Orders of August 1883 clarified the position regarding the wearing by ORs of badges for swordsmanship and shooting:

'The Troops Badges for Shooting and Swordsmanship to be worn for one year only, and will be Silver Cross-Swords or Muskets. Regimental Badges for Swordsmanship or Shooting for the current year, Gold Badge with a Gold Crown above it, to be worn for one year only. Yeomen who have won the Regimental Sword or Shooting Competition any 3 years of their service may wear the Cross-Swords or Muskets with Crown in Silver, for the remainder of their service. Any Yeoman found wearing a badge to which he is not entitled after the promulgation of this Order will be fined 5/-.'

Orders of April 1888 introduced the 'Dartmouth Badges'. These were silver lace long-service badges of the style in use by the regulars, worn on the lower left arm. They were donated to the regiment by the Earl of Dartmouth, and all privates and NCOs were eligible to wear them. They were awarded as follows: 4yrs. – 1 badge; 6 yrs. – 2 badges; 10 yrs. – 3 badges; 15 yrs. – 4 badges; 25 yrs. – 4 badges with 2 (five-pointed) silver stars upon them; 40 yrs. – 4 badges with 2 silver stars upon them and 1 (four-pointed) gold star above. This last arrangement can be seen being worn by TQMS Horne in Fig.24.

Marching Order for ORs was described in the same order as:

'Helmet and Plume, Tunic, Pants, High Boots and Spurs, Pouch Belt, Sword and Belts, Carbine and Cape on Saddle, the Cape to be rolled 18 inches, placed at back of saddle, and buckles of straps in line on top of cape, the loose ends of straps to be towards the seat.'

It further stipulates that, 'No Parcels, Caps, Whips or Canes to be carried on the Saddle...' and that, 'The Plumes to be clean, and small at the top.'

By the 1880s, a scarlet pillbox cap appears to have replaced the kepi for undress wear. For ORs, the decoration of this cap had become in itself a badge of rank. Privates had a plain black braid band with black piping in the crown welt, a four-part figure in black piping on the top, and black button. Corporals wore a large silver embroidered knot upon the band, the knot having small flecks of scarlet woven into it. Serjeants wore a silver band with a blue line running through the centre. Staff serjeants wore a cap simi-

Fig. 34: Field Officer's Tunic c. 1883-1914. Note the collar laced all round, and the Artillery pattern field officer's sleeve and cuff ornamentation. It will also be observed that the distinctive gilt picker plate on silver lace is of oval shape and has bodkin headed pickers. *Regimental collection*

lar to that of the officers, with a silver lace band, silver piping in the crown welt, but with a button and simplified eight-part decoration in silver piping on the top.

Although no exact dates have been found for the changes, the undress uniform of the officers appears to have gradually changed during the 1870s and 80s. Headgear was standardised from the several types to be seen in the group photograph of 1861 to the scarlet, silver laced pillbox cap, with a six-part silver piped figure without button, on top. By the 1880s, the earlier type of braided frock coat gave way to another Regular style – of the type with broad black tapes across the breast and the heavy figuring on the cuff. Also by this time, the plain blue stable jacket had given way to another Regular style, edged all round with silver lace, with small silver ball buttons down the front, as worn by Captain Davenport in Fig.22. In mess dress, a distinctive scarlet waistcoat was worn beneath the open stable jacket. The waistcoat was edged with silver lace, and had the small silver ball buttons down the front, and was further decorated with six silver embroidered Stafford knots down each side, each one traced with silver Russia braid. The pockets were also traced with the same braid, with a knot beneath each (see Fig.25).

The Hawkes pattern book of officers uniforms for 1883 refers to an early innovation for a yeomanry regiment – a blue serge jumper, or frock. Beyond stating that it had no outside pockets, no further details were given, and no contemporary illustrations of it are known to the authors. Another ranks' version of this new undress item was apparently introduced at roughly the same time. This plain six-button blue frock with cutaway skirts and scarlet collar was being worn with overalls or pantaloons for drill purposes by the 1890s. A photograph of the Lichfield Troop (Fig.28) shows that Staff Serjeants' frocks were ornamented with silver shoulder cords, silver lace on the cuffs, and silver cord all round the collar. Other NCOs wear the same unadorned garment as the troopers. Interestingly, the photograph (Fig.27) used by Cooper-King shows a staff serjeant wearing the same type of frock, but differently embellished.

The 1883 pattern book also gives officers dress overalls and pantaloons as having double silver lace stripes, and undress ones with double scarlet stripes. It describes the officers' cloak as blue, of the regulation pattern, lined with scarlet, with a back strap having two flap buttons, and a scarlet collar, fastened with rose clasps.

The black Albert helmet had continued as the dress headgear of the Regiment since 1850. By this time, however, the acanthus plume socket had changed to a spear point type, and the acorn finial on top of the plume had changed to a flat rosette. The 1893 training, however, was to be the last time the helmet was worn, and, although it would appear that some consideration was given to introducing a metal helmet of the contemporary heavy cavalry type to replace the Albert[4], in the following year, the uniform of the Regiment received the final 'crowning' item required to complete the hussar style it had been moving towards since the introduction of the six-row tunic.

Fig. 35: Officer's Full Dress Tunic *c.* 1883-1914. Collar and sleeve braided according to rank below that of Field Officer. *Regimental collection*

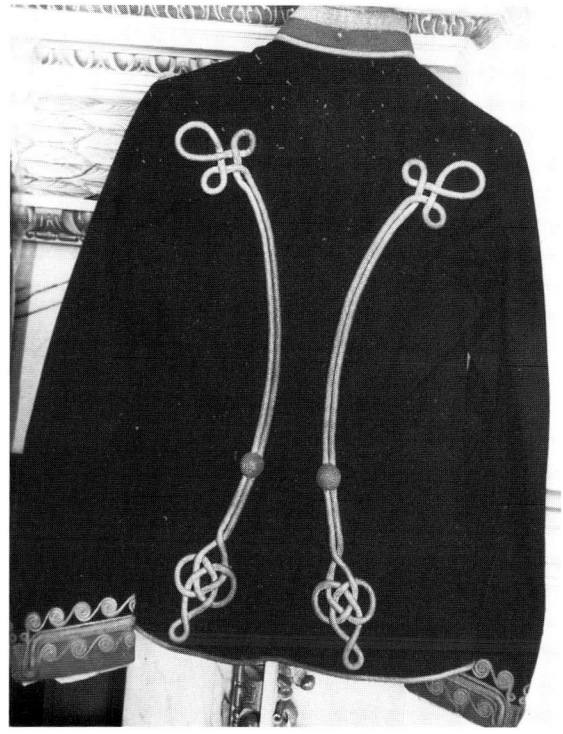

Footnotes:

1. Although Norie, in a large painting of various uniforms of the regiment (in the Regimental collection), shows an 'Austrian' style helmet, of the type mentioned here, in use between the departure of the 'Tarleton' and the adoption of the Shako, the authors, after much consideration, feel that this is, in fact, artistic licence, and no other evidence exists that such a pattern of helmet was worn by the Regiment. Errors are apparent elsewhere in the painting, which, in the

authors' opinion, brings its overall dependability as a reference into doubt.
2. The pattern book of c.1848 held in the National Army Museum.
3. *Yeomanry and Other Sabretaches,* MHS Special Number, 1988.
4. Reference W.Y. Carman, *Headdresses of The British Army.*

A Note on Shabracks

A shabrack is shown in an illustration of a mounted officer on a sheet music cover of the 'The Queen's Own Royal Staffordshire Yeomanry Cavalry Galop', published in Lichfield in about 1870. However, whilst the uniform is tolerably correct, the shabrack is felt by the authors to be the product of artistic licence. Other than the description given of the shabrack worn with the first uniform of the Regiment, and Simkin's later interpretations of the uniforms of 1816 and 1838, where shabracks are shown which appear to be directly based upon contemporary regular Light Dragoon patterns, the music cover is the only depiction known to the authors showing a design for a later period. No other contemporary written or pictorial evidence has in fact been found of the Regiment ever having had shabracks. Certainly no actual examples have survived. What must be the earliest surviving photograph of a mounted officer in review order, a regrettably poor quality one taken about 1880 of Major Thomas Thorneycroft, shows, where one would expect to see a shabrack for this order of dress, the plain black sheepskin with scarlet scalloped edges.

All this leads the authors to the conclusion that, other than the possible exception of the type described for 1794, it is unlikely that the Regiment ever actually used a shabrack.

Chapter II

Historical Notes 1894 to 1914

In 1894, during the permanent duty at Lichfield, the centenary of the Regiment was celebrated, the Regiment being, fittingly, under the (4th) Duke of Sutherland, whose ancestor, Earl Gower (later in 1833 created Duke of Sutherland) had raised the corps. The training, which commenced on 22 May, was a brigade one, the Warwickshire Yeomanry marching into Lichfield the same day. The Duke of Sutherland acted as brigadier, being the senior of the two regimental commanders, and handed his own regiment over to Lt.-Colonel Talbot. At this training, the Staffordshire wore for the first time a Hussar busby with scarlet bag and white plume and lines.

On 28 May, an address from the Mayor and Corporation of the city of Lichfield was presented ceremonially to the Regiment, in honour of the centenary, on the lawns in front of Yeomanry House, the Regimental Headquarters, to which address the Colonel made a suitable reply.

On 29 May, Colonel R.S. Liddle, late of the 10th Hussars, officially inspected the Regiment, with the Warwickshire Yeomanry, in brigade work. During the evening, H.R.H. the Prince of Wales arrived at Lichfield to make the centenary inspection. He was met at the station by Colonel the Duke of Sutherland, whose guest he was, the Honorary Colonel (the Marquis of Anglesey) and General Julian Hall, commanding the District. The Prince was received by the Staffordshire Yeomanry, who, with their band, were drawn up outside the station, and was escorted by a field officer's escort of 100 picked men and horses, with six officers, under the command of Sir Reginald Hardy, Bart. On 30 May, the Prince of Wales, accompanied by a travelling escort under Lieut. Ralph Sneyd, arrived at the racecourse on Whittington Heath to inspect the Regiment, which was drawn up in brigade with the Warwickshire Yeomanry. The Royal Standard of the Regiment was brought out for the occasion and was carried by Quartermaster Horne, who was complimented by the Prince. Quartermaster Horne was 68 years old and for 51 of those years he had served in the Staffordshire Yeomanry (Fig.24).

Fig. 36: Forage Caps. (a) Officer's forage cap c. 1883-1903. (b) Warrant Officer's and Staff Serjeant's forage cap c. 1883-1905. Details in text. *Regimental collection*

In May 1895 the annual training was again carried out at Lichfield and Captain Lovelace Stamer, 16th (The Queen's) Lancers was appointed Adjutant of the 8th Brigade. In the same year, the Headquarters of the Regiment moved from Yeomanry House to the ancient Friary and grounds in the centre of Lichfield, where the officers and staff had convenient quarters and where the regimental stores were also established. The enrolled strength of the four squadrons in this year amounted to 362 of all ranks.

The 1896 training commenced on 13 May at Lichfield, the Regiment mustering 312 men out of 328 enrolled. The inspecting officer was Colonel H.S. Gough, C.M.G., Assistant Adjutant-General of Cavalry.

On 8 January 1897 an escort under Captain A.H. Heath was provided from the Queen's Own Royal Regiment of Staffordshire Yeomanry Cavalry for the Prince and Princess of Wales, who were staying with Colonel the Duke of Sutherland at Trentham Hall.

The Regiment met at Lichfield on 11 May for the 1897 training, and on the 19th, Colonel J.D.P. French (afterwards General Sir John French), one of the Brigadiers Commanding Cavalry Brigades under the recent Organisation Scheme, made the inspection. During this training special attention was devoted to reconnaissance and outpost duty and, in accordance with the new regulations, there were few parade movements and no addresses, either from the inspecting or commanding officer.

The Regiment was now armed with .303 Martini-Metford carbines and secured third place in the Bisley Inter-Yeomanry Cup at the National Rifle Meeting. The effective strength of the Regiment in 1897 was 303 of all ranks, the lowest strength the Regiment had ever fallen to in modern times.

In June 1897, a detachment of the Queen's Own Royal Staffordshire Yeomanry Cavalry journeyed to London and took part in the Diamond Jubilee celebrations of Her Majesty Queen Victoria.

On 23 March 1898 Lt.-Col. J. Heath succeeded Colonel the Duke of Sutherland in the command of the Regiment. Annual training was again held at Lichfield and the corps was inspected by Field Marshal Viscount Wolseley. This year the Staffordshire Yeomanry were second in the Hythe Inter-Yeomanry Cup and took the same placing in the N.R.A. Inter-Yeomanry Cup. The Honorary Colonel the Marquis of Anglesey died on 13 October 1898. He was succeeded by Colonel T.J. Levett on 5 February 1899. With the appointment on 1 September 1899 of Captain R.C. Stephen of the 14th (The King's) Hussars as Adjutant, there began a period of a little over ten years in which three officers in succession from that distinguished Regiment served in the adjutancy of the Staffordshire Yeomanry.

During the South African War the Staffordshire Yeomanry served with distinction, having answered the call to arms early in January 1900 by forming a company for active service. Captain W. Bromley-Davenport was selected to command the company and was accompanied by Lieuts. W. Moat, T.A. Wight-Boycott, H. Cecil Gardner and G.A. Clay, all of the Regiment. Under the direction of Colonel James Heath and with the assistance the Adjutant, Captain Stephen, the 6th (Staffordshire) Company of Imperial Yeomanry was quickly raised. The contingent, which sailed from Liverpool on 26 January 1900 as part of Colonel Blair's 4th Battalion of Imperial Yeomanry, included 64 Yeomen and 50 civilians and Volunteers who were specially enlisted in the Staffordshire Yeomanry to complete. On Good Friday 1900, a relief draft was sent out by the regiment to fill up vacancies in the Service Company in South Africa (Figs.38-42).

When the time came, in May 1901, after months of hard work in the field, only half the original strength of the company were mustered, some 60 men under the command of Captain H.C. Gardner who embarked at Capetown together with their late Captain, Lt.-Col. Bromley-Davenport, who had been promoted to the command of the 4th Battalion. Captain T.A.

18

Fig. 37: Officer's Field Service Cap *c.* 1898-*c.* 1903. *Regimental collection*

Fig. 38: Slouch Hat, All Ranks, *c.* 1900-1903. Drab hat and pagri. *Regimental collection*

Wight-Boycott had also been appointed major of the Battalion.

In Lord Roberts' despatches of 10 September 1900 Major Bromley-Davenport and Captain T.A. Wight-Boycott were mentioned, both officers, on the Commander-in-Chief's recommendation, receiving the D.S.O. Three members of the contingent died from wounds received in action and 11 others of disease. Lieutenant Moat and 50 other members of the squadron were invalided and some four others remained in South Africa doing duty in the police. No less than six obtained commissioned rank, one of whom, Private R.B. Bagallay (invalided home), was given a commission in the Queen's Own Royal Staffordshire Yeomanry.

On Saturday 8 June 1901 the first contingent returned to England and, journeying on Sunday from Southampton where they had disembarked, were met at Lichfield railway station by the Mayor and Corporation of the city, together with the High Sheriff of the County and several of the officers and men of the Queen's Own Staffordshire Yeomanry. On 19 October 1901 the members of the Service Squadron, together with the Staffordshire Volunteers returned from South Africa, were presented with war medals by the Earl of Dartmouth, Lord Lieutenant of Staffordshire, at the Borough Hall, Stafford, in the presence of a distinguished company.

For the Home Service unit, the annual training of 1900 was delayed as a result of the raising of the service contingent and did not take place until July; the Regiment assembled on the 17th in Keele Park and for the first time in its history was placed under canvas. The troopers went through a period of strict military discipline and duty, gaining themselves the utmost credit under the most trying conditions, and elicited the warm praise of Colonel the Hon. R.T. Lawley, the commanding officer of the 7th Hussars, who was the inspecting officer.

On 2 February 1901 the Lichfield Troop, with the other local forces, attended a memorial service for her late Majesty Queen Victoria at Lichfield Cathedral.

Another draft was sent out in 1901 to fill up the 6th (Staffordshire) Company to its strength, and a second company of Imperial Yeomanry, numbered the 106th (Staffordshire) was also raised and sent out to join the 4th Battalion of Imperial Yeomanry in South Africa.

In July 1902, the two Staffordshire Companies (new 6th and 106th), after hard trekking work in the numerous drives that had concluded the war, embarked for England, arriving home on 11 August.

In May 1901, the Queen's Own Royal Staffordshire Regiment of Yeomanry Cavalry was re-organised with the other units as Imperial Yeomanry. The future training was to be half that of Light Horse and half that of Mounted Infantry, the arms being Lee-Enfield magazine rifles and bayonets instead of swords and carbines, but the swords were afterwards allowed to be retained for ceremonial purposes. The new establishment was now ordered to be four squadrons and a machine gun detachment, with a total establishment of all ranks of 596, the officers including an adjutant, one being allowed once more to each regiment, numbering some 27, and consisted of 1 Lieutenant-Colonel in command, 1 Major (second in command), 4 Captains, 17 Lieutenants and Second Lieutenants, 1 Adjutant, 1 Quartermaster, 1 Medical Officer and 1 Veterinary officer; later, four more majors were allowed, the number of subalterns being reduced by four to 13. The Regiment being a 4-squadron one, the old recruiting centres were still maintained. New allowances were also issued. The Inter-Yeomanry Cup fell to the regimental team (Fig.44) who secured first place at Bisley this year. On June 18th the Regiment assembled at Hagley Park, Rugeley, for 14 days' training and were inspected by Colonel E.R. Courtenay.

On 15 January 1902 Captain T.E.L. Hill Whitson, 14th Hussars was appointed Adjutant. The Queen's Own Royal Staffordshire Imperial Yeomanry furnished an escort for King Edward VII on 24 February, on his departure from Rangemore, Buton. On 25 February, Colonel Heath retired from the command, and Lord Bagot, the senior major also retiring, the command passed to Major Sir Reginald Hardy, Bart., who was gazetted to the command of 11 March 1902.,

On 1 May the Regiment provided an escort to HRH the Duke of Connaught, and on the 29th of the same month, to HRH Prince Christian. Hagley Park was the scene of the 1902 camp, which began on 12 May. In August, a detachment of the Staffordshire Yeomanry journeyed to London and took part in the Coronation celebrations. At Bisley, the third place in the Inter-Yeomanry Cup fell to the Regiment. In this year, the four squadrons returned 487 of all ranks.

The 1903 training was held at Trentham Park, commencing on 11 May; Colonel the Earl of Errol inspected the Regiment. On July 3rd, the Regiment furnished an escort to HRH Princess Henry of Battenberg at Wolverhampton. The enrolled strength in 1903 was 484 officers and men.

In 1904, the encampment for training was held on the Freeford Estate, near Lichfield, the duty commencing on 11 May. This year the Regiment was officially inspected by Colonel J. Fowle, 21st Lancers. On 21st December in a Special Army Order the Queen's Own Royal Staffordshire Yeomanry were granted permission by His Majesty the King to bear 'South Africa, 1900-01' on their appointments.

On 15 January 1905 Captain E.T. Jameson, 14th Hussars, was appointed Adjutant. The 1905 permanent duty was performed under canvas at Chartley between 16th and 31st May and the Regiment was inspected by Colonel Little, C.B., District Staff Officer of Yeomanry.

Colonel Sir Reginald Hardy, Bart. resigned on 13 March 1906 and on 7 April Lt.-Col. A.H. Heath was gazetted to the command, Lt.-Col. W. Bromley-Davenport, DSO, being appointed second in command. Himley was the place selected for the 1906 camp. The Regiment in 1906 was still organised in four squadrons, but now with an establishment of 476 of all ranks, with headquarters and stores still at the Friary, Lichfield; 'A' Squadron (Lichfield and Walsall) with headquarters at Lichfield; 'B' Squadron (Newcastle and Stafford) with headquarters at Newcastle 'C' Squadron (Burton and Uttoxeter) with headquarters at Burton; 'D' Squadron (Himley and Wolverhampton) with headquarters at Himley, with the addition of a machine gun, ambulance and signalling sections with headquarters at Lichfield.

Trentham Park was the location chosen for the annual training in 1907. The following year, the Staffordshire Yeomanry became part of the newly created Territorial Force and joined the North Midlands Mounted Brigade, together with the Lincolnshire and Leicestershire Yeomanry.

By around 1908-1910, the Regiment had organised a Musical Ride, which became very popular and was highly successful, appearing at camp and at such shows as the Wolverhampton Floral Fete. The members carried lances and wore their full dress tunics, with busbies, blue riding pantaloons and knee boots issued from a small supply held at H.Q.

Trentham Park was again selected as the site of the annual training in 1909. On 15 January 1910 Captain H.B. Towse of the Royal Scots Greys succeeded Captain E.J. Jameson as Adjutant on completion of his period of engagement. In April the same year, Lt.-Col. A.H. Heath retired from command and, on the 7th of that month, was succeeded by Lt.-Col. W. Bromley-Davenport, DSO. A brigade camp was held this year at Croxton Park, Leicester, and a photograph (not reproduced here) depicts all three regiments of the North Midland Mounted Brigade at a combined Church Parade.

The year 1911 was an eventful one, being Coronation year. Annual training was carried out at Keele Park and a detachment of 25 ORs under the

Fig. 39: South African War. Group from the Himley Troop. Back row (l. to r.) Privates Jones, Munday and Cartwright. These volunteers, shown prior to departure for the front, are wearing slouch hats, khaki mixture frocks, cord pantaloons, khaki puttees and ankle boots with hunting spurs, foot straps and leather shields. Note the web bandoliers. *Photograph courtesy of* The Black Country Bugle

Fig. 40: Captain W. Bromley-Davenport, 6th (Staffordshire) Company, 5th Battalion Imperial Yeomanry, at the Front, 1900. A rare photograph of Captain Bromley-Davenport actually in the field. He wears the slouch hat with Stafford knot badge (see Fig. 43), khaki frock and Sam Browne belt. A binocular case is visible. *Regimental collection*

command of Captain G.P. Heywood paraded dismounted in London for street lining duties on 22 and 23 June wearing the complete old Hussar full dress. (See Part 10 of this series for further details of the Coronation.) On 1 July 1911 a guard of honour was furnished by the Regiment at the opening of the new Drill Hall at Wolverhampton (Fig.57).

On 27 March 1912 Captain A.C. Watson of the 7th (The Queen's Own) Hussars took over the Adjutancy until before the outbreak of the First World War. Annual camp was held at Barton under Needwood in 1912 followed by Towcester in 1913.

In 1914, the Regimental Headquarters are listed as Bailey Street, Stafford, with 'A' Squadron headquarters at Walsall and drill stations at West Bromwich, Tamworth, Lichfield and Sutton Coldfield; 'B' Squadron headquarters at Stoke on Trent, with drill stations at Stafford, Leek, Cannock and Newcastle-under-Lyme; 'C' Squadron headquarters at Burton on Trent with a drill station at Uttoxeter; 'D' Squadron headquarters at Wolverhampton with a drill station at Himley. The Regiment formed part of the North Midlands Mounted Brigade, with headquarters at 7 Magazine Square, Leicester.

The last annual camp of the Staffordshire Yeomanry to be held prior to the First World War took place at Patshull Park in May-June 1914.

As has been the practice throughout this series, due to pressure of space no attempt has been made to cover either the South African War records or the details of the uniform and accoutrements used by the Staffordshire I.Y. during that campaign. However, Figs.38-42 refer to this subject and have appropriate captions.

Uniform Details 1894-1914

Full Dress

As earlier stated, a new crowning item was required to complete the Staffordshires' Hussar style of uniform; this was a busby, which was introduced in time for the annual training at Lichfield in 1894. It was of the pattern which had been officially approved for regulars in November 1887. For the officers (Fig.31), it was of black sable with scarlet cloth bag or 'fly' on the right side, which was traced around the edge and down the centre with fine silver braid; there was a silver gimp button at the bottom edge of the centre row. The plume, which was of upright white egret feathers rising from a white vulture feather base, had a silver retaining ring which was mounted in a silver four-leaf holder with a corded ball base located near the front edge of the headdress. There was a silver gimp boss embedded in the fur near the top front edge. Three rows of silver cord cap line encircled the headdress diagonally. The corded silver metal curb chin chain was mounted on a red Morocco leather backing. From 1902 there were new plumes of white ostrich feathers, the base feathers remaining as before.

The ORs had basically the same pattern of busby (Fig.32), but of sealskin, with a shorter plume of white horsehair, white braid boss and lines and white metal fittings (Fig.32). Officers and men wore the cap lines in the same fashion, which was with the body section of the lines from the cap around the neck, secured by runners and looped with the egg mould finials on the right breast near the shoulder (Fig.31).

From 1894 to 1914, the other items of full dress described under 'Uniform 1881-1893' were little altered. Some further details and notes of subsequent minor changes which took place will, however, be of interest. The officers' full dress tunics retained the old distinctive features, namely the braiding according to rank on the collars, cuffs and sleeves of the field officers in the Royal Artillery fashion (Fig.34) and the figuring around the Austrian knots over the cuffs of all officers below field rank, which was in 6th Dragoon Guards style (Fig.35). Another feature which was apparently retained up to 1914 was the silver staff cord for all the loops and braiding of the officers' tunics, instead of the more widely-used chain gimp lace. The silver plaited shoulder cords were of the pattern adopted in 1880-1881 and bore gold embroidered badges of rank. In 1894, Hussar-style boot bosses, which were of silver chain gimp and were detachable, were introduced for wear on the front of the officers knee boots. About the same date, tailor's notes inform us that 'blue tight fitting "Hussar" pantaloons with silver stripes and Hessian boots' were authorised for Levees and Balls; the use of these items was discontinued by a memo dated 13 February 1903. With regard to the other netherwear, both the silver laced 'Dress' pantaloons and the overalls continued to be worn for some years, but were discontinued after 1901, being replaced by the undress items with double scarlet cloth side stripes. The handsome velvet pouch (Fig.7) and silver oak leaf laced belt (Fig.34) with its distinctive 'gilt' front ornaments were retained until 1914 and the pouch can just be seen in a 1911 photograph showing the rear view of an officer (Fig.57). The silver laced sword slings were also retained but, unfortunately, the beautiful silver laced velvet sabretache (Fig.18) was abolished in 1902.

As with virtually all the Yeomanry corps, the officers' swords were of no fixed pattern and in the main appear to be of the Light Cavalry officers 1822 pattern (Fig.58) or at times (from about 1897 onwards) the scroll hilted Cavalry officers 1896 pattern. This remained the case up to 1914. In both cases the knots were of gold cord and the olivets of gold.

A most interesting entry in a memo to tailors dated 13 February 1903 refers to a 'white helmet' and indicates that it would replace the busby and lines after the 1903 training. Exhaustive enquiries have failed to trace any evidence of this being anything other than 'under consideration'. In the Orderly Book entries dated 19 May 1903 is listed (presumably for escort duty) 'Officers Full Dress, Tunic, busby and lines, plume, white gloves, pantaloons with red stripes, jack boots with spurs, sword in frog on saddle, no sabretache, silver sword and pouch belt with full dress pouch, gold sword knot, horse plume, headrope, cloak on rear on saddle.'

After a lot of consideration and uncertainty, the question of the future of the full dress for all ranks appears to have been settled about 1906-1907. The officers were to retain the Hussar kit for Levee Dress and for very important ceremonial duties. Otherwise, for Church Parade and other occasions when a smart uniform was required, from about 1907 to 1914 the officers wore the forage cap and blue serge kit described in 'Undress 1894-1914'. Although not as handsome as the old Hussar kit, the substitute was, nevertheless, smart and practical (Fig.55).

Following the introduction of the busby in 1894, little alteration in the full dress of the men took place before about 1903. The appearance of the ORs after the busbys had been served out is shown in Figs.32 and 33. About 1903, it was decided to change the pattern of the men's tunics, which were still of the 1881 style, to one based exactly on that of the contemporary regular Hussars, except that the knots, loops and braiding were of white cord (silver for W.O.'s and Staff Sergeants) instead of yellow, and the collars and cuffs had scarlet cloth facings; the NCO's chevrons were of silver lace on a scarlet backing. It is possible to see both the old and new patterns of tunic worn concurrently in a group photograph of 'C' Squadron at

Fig. 41: Private J. Waters *c, 1900.* Private Waters is shown mounted, on service in South Africa. Note his long Lee Enfield rifle, bandolier and the blue cloak strapped to the front of the saddle. *Regimental collection*

Fig. 42: Foreign Service Helmet, South African War, *c.* 1900-01. Drab covered helmet and pagri, patch of blue-red-blue stripes, white metal knot. Versions are known bearing the figure '6' above the patch. *Regimental collection*

Trentham camp in 1903 (Fig.45), when the process of reclothing the men was obviously under way. The new tunic can be seen more clearly in Fig.50 which shows a trumpeter in about 1907-1908. His trumpet cords, incidentally, were as for a Royal Regiment, that is, mixed red, blue and yellow. A detailed view of the front and rear ornamentation on this garment is shown in Figs.48 and 49.

From an entry dated January 1903 in the Orderly Books we learn that, for mounted duties in full dress, the NCOs and men would wear 'Tunic, busby and lines with plume, white gloves, "blue" (recruits khaki) pantaloons, jack boots (recruits ankle boots) and spurs, no belts, sword in frog on saddle, cloak in rear of saddle, rifle in bucket, saddlery complete with pipeclayed headrope. Men who have not got busbies will wear forage caps. Bandoliers and sword belts

21

Fig. 43: Plate of Badges, Shoulder Titles, etc. Officers wore No. 4 in silver with gilt knot on the scarlet field service cap (Fig. 37) 1898-1903. No. 6 was worn by officers in silver with gilt knot on the forage cap from 1903. From 1908 they wore it in bronze on the service dress cap (Fig. 59).

No. 2[1] was worn as follows: (a) in white metal (w/m)[2] by other ranks on the scarlet field service cap from 1898; by all ranks of 6th and 106th I.Y. Companies 1900-02 on the khaki helmet (Fig. 42); by all ranks of 6th and 106th I.Y. Companies 1900-02 and of the regiment 1901-03, with a scarlet backing, which did not protrude beyond the edges of the badge, on the turned-up side of the slouch hat (Fig. 38); by other ranks on the forage cap 1906-13 (Figs. 47 & 50) and on the service dress cap 1907-08. (b) By other ranks in gilding metal (g.m.) on the service dress cap 1908-13[3].

No. 9 replaced No. 2 as the other ranks' cap badge in 1913: in w/m on the forage cap (Fig. 61) and in g.m. on the service dress cap[4]. A badge of the same design and materials as No. 4, measuring 34mm by 22mm, was worn on the scarlet collar of the officer's blue frock from 1901 (Fig. 44) and on the universal pattern mess dress from 1903. Collar badges were not worn by officers in service dress or at all by other ranks during the period covered by this book.

No. 5 was worn on the shoulder straps of the embellished khaki jacket 1904-08 in w/m. From 1908 No. 7, the standard pattern Yeomanry shoulder title[4], was worn in g.m. by other ranks on the universal pattern khaki jacket and greatcoat. No. 8 was worn on the shoulder chains of the other ranks' optional blue frock 1908-14 (Fig. 61).

In 1859 the regiment adopted No. 1, a semi-domed button, with Victorian crown over a strap, without buckle, worded as No. 4, surrounding the knot. This was worn by officers in silver and by other ranks in w/m, with change after Queen Victoria's death in 1901 to the Tudor or 'King's' crown pattern, i.e. with rounded arches.

No. 3 however, from 1908, on the standard pattern service dress jacket and overcoat officers wore No. 3 in gilt and other ranks wore the universal, royal arms, button in g.m.

The other ranks of the regiment were unusual in wearing large semi-domed buttons with regimental device, Nos. 1 & 3, with hussar tunics and also in adopting badges bearing the Victorian crown, Nos. 8 & 9, some years after Queen Victoria's death; particularly as the officers had worn a cap badge with the Tudor crown, No. 6, since 1903.

Footnotes
1. A badge of the same size and design was already worn, as a collar badge, by the South Staffordshire Regiment (in g.m. by regular battalions and in w/m by volunteer battalions).
2. Known as German Silver until the 1914-18 War.
3. T. F. Regulations 1908, para 554.
4. T. F. Regulations 1912, para 487.
5. T. F. Regulations 1908, para 552 and Appendix 16.

K. Hook collection

Fig. 44: The Staffordshire Yeomanry Shooting Team, Winners of the Inter Yeomanry Cup, Bisley, 1901. Scarlet field service caps are featured here with blue serge Dismounted Drill Order. The officer (seated, right) wears a full dress pouch belt. *Collection of N. Mander*

to be brought into camp'. It further orders that 'All yeomen when out of camp must appear properly dressed, viz. tunics and lines, forage cap, overalls, Wellington boots and spurs, gloves and whip'. At the same time, reference to swords is made as follows: 'In future, swords will only be carried when mounted by Officers, Permanent Staff, SSMs, SQMs, Sergeant Farriers and Trumpeters'. Guards were ordered to mount in 'Review Order with rifles and slings'.

As in the case of the officers, following much uncertainty during the years 1901-1904 the question of the full dress for the ORs appears finally to have been settled between 1906-1907. The Hussar tunics of the new pattern were retained, as were the blue overalls with double scarlet stripes, Wellington boots and spurs, white lines and white gloves, but the busbies were withdrawn, although a small number were retained in stock for special occasions. The same applied to the blue riding pantaloons and knee boots, which were no longer worn. However, some sets were kept in store at RHQ for issue to the Musical Ride and for such duties as mounted escort should the occasion arise. In 1906, blue and scarlet staff pattern peaked forage caps, as worn by the officers from 1903, were now served out to the men (Fig 47 and 50); for badges, see Fig.43. The cap replaced both the busby and the old pillbox cap. The new headdress, together with the articles listed above, which may be seen in Fig. 61 and 62 now constituted both the ORs' full and walking out dress, continuing to do so up to 1914.

Undress

In undress, the scarlet pill box caps, stable jackets, frock coats and other items described in 'Uniform 1881-1893' continued to be worn by the officers, although by the late 1890s the stable jacket had been subjected to some slight alteration and eventually became confined to officers' mess dress. By about 1895-6, a serge frock was in use; it is described in tailor's notes as 'blue serge "Norfolk", 2½in pleats down fronts and centre back, a 2in serge waist belt with silver buckle in front. Shoulder straps of same material as jacket with regimental buttons'. In about 1897, this item was exchanged for one 'cut as patrol, pleats down fronts and back, a 2in serge belt with one-prong buckle, four outside patch pockets with pleats, flaps and buttons, five small buttons down front and plain sleeves'. As yet there was no mention of collar badges or shoulder chains. A further version of the frock (Fig.45) appeared about 1900-1901.

This garment is recorded as being of the '1896 pattern with scarlet stand collar, shoulder chains of solid nickel with silver metal rank badges and silver collar ornaments, five small buttons down front, and two at the hind seam of the blue pointed cuffs, four plain patch packets (but pleats have been noted) with pointed flaps, buttons on the breast pockets only'. There were longish cut side vents or slits. The officers' black braided frock coat, although ordered to be discontinued by memo to the tailors dated 13 February 1903, continued to be worn unofficially by some officers, when off duty, for sports days and Sundays in camp up to 1914. It may be seen in use by Lieutenant-Colonel Bromley-Davenport in about 1908 in Fig.52.

On 24 February 1894 the Orderly Books record that 'the officers' black leather (undress) pouch belt was no longer to be worn'. A further memo to tailors in 1903 states that 'black belts, pouch and sword knot should be discontinued along with the red field service cap and frock coat'. The field service cap seems to have appeared about 1898-9; it was of all scarlet cloth; there was silver piping on all the seams and flaps, two small buttons in front of the flaps and a badge was worn on the body of the cap at the left (Fig.37). This headdress does not appear to have been very popular and had a short official life.

The undress netherwear between 1894 and 1914 was, for mounted duties, dark blue pantaloons with double ⅞in scarlet cloth side stripes, black knee boots and spurs; during the years 1901-1903 blue puttees and ankle boots were substituted. For dismounted duties, blue overalls with the same cloth stripes as the pants were worn over Wellington boots and box spurs. In the post 1900 period, plain blue serge trousers and black laced ankle boots (Fig.56) were also worn off duty in camp.

For the training of 1901 held at Hagley Park, the regimental Orderly Books entry for 22 June reveals that full dress of 'tunics and busbies' would not be required and officers were ordered to wear overalls, Wellington boots and spurs, serge jacket (blue frock), hats (slouch), silver pouch belts, black pouches, brown gloves, swords and black sabretaches for Church Parade. The reference to black sabretaches is interesting as this was no doubt the last use of this item, which became obsolete and is deleted from the 1902 orders.

In 1903, a smart new forage cap (Fig.45) was introduced for officers to replace the pill box. It was of the peaked staff

Fig. 45: Officers and N.C.Os, 'C' Squadron, Trentham Park Camp, 1903. The officers wear the new peaked forage caps and blue serge frocks. Two are dressed for Mounted Drill Order in pantaloons and knee boots, while one officer has off duty blue trousers. Forage caps of the old pill box pattern are worn by the N.C.Os, with the exception of one, who has a field service cap. Their full dress tunics are either of the 1881 pattern or the new type which was in the process of being issued (see Figs. 48, 49). *Regimental collection*

pattern, of dark blue cloth with a scarlet band and piping round the crown seam and a black patent leather peak and chin strap held by two small buttons. The peaks of the field officers were distinguished by a row of silver wire braiding round the edge. The cap badge is shown in Fig.43.

From about 1906-7 onwards, the Hussar full dress was reserved for special duties only and was generally replaced by Parade Dress (Fig.55) for the officers until 1914. The parade dress consisted of the forage cap described above (at times with a white top cover), the blue serge frock with scarlet collar and shoulder chains and blue overalls with double scarlet side stripes worn over Wellington boots with box spurs. The full dress silver laced pouch belt and velvet pouch were worn, together with silver laced sword slings and a sword with gold cord knot and olivet. White wrist gloves completed the uniform.

Between the 1894 and 1905, the ORs continued to wear the scarlet pill box forage caps exactly as described under 'Uniform 1881-1893'. Alternatively, from around 1899-1900, a field service cap of the same Austrian shape described for the officers' undress made its appearance (Fig.44). It was all scarlet, but lacked the silver piping and bore a different badge (Fig.43). It is, however, quite likely that WOs and Staff Sergeants had some distinguishing silver trimming. From January 1903, the field service cap was relegated to being worn for fatigues by the men.

Photographs of about 1898-9 show that the O.Rs had been issued with a new pattern of blue serge frock (Fig. 47), which now featured two plain breast patch pockets with silver buttons on the pointed flaps. There were five similar buttons down the front of the garment and two at the hind seam of each plain cuff. It seems likely that the old scarlet collars were retained on the new serges. The narrower shoulder cords were of scarlet worsted, with a small silver button at the top; sergeants and above were distinguished by silver cords. Rank chevrons were of silver lace throughout for N.C.O.s. However, a photograph which was published in the *Navy and Army Illustrated* for 25 February 1898 shows a mounted parade in which all ranks wear pill box caps. The officers have serge frocks and full dress pouch belts, but the men are wearing stable jackets

and black pouch belts. The photograph may, of course, have been taken a year of so earlier, or it may simply have been thought appropriate for the men to wear something smarter than frocks for the photograph. All ranks wore pantaloons and knee boots and there were steel chains in the horse kit. The officers' chargers have white throat plumes.

With reference to Hagley Park camp, the Orderly Books for 11 May 1901 order that 'every NCO and Trooper going into camp at Hagley Park this year will provide himself with a small box or valise to contain all extra kit, *i.e.* 2 serge jackets, 1 pair overalls with stripes, 1 pair blue serge trousers, 1 pair Wellington boots and spurs, 1 pair lace boots and such other things as are necessary for camp. Tunics and Busbies will not be required'. For Church Parade, the 'NCOs and men will wear Wellington boots and spurs, serge jackets (blue frocks), hats (slouch), ban-

Fig. 46: Group of O.Rs, May 1905. These O.Rs all wear the *c.* 1904 pattern scarlet embellished service dress. Although two have the official old pattern pill box forage cap which was soon to be replaced, three of the men wear the obsolete and short-lived field service cap. *Author's collection*

Fig. 47: Private, Mounted Drill Order, *c.* 1907. This subject appears in the 1906 pattern forage cap and the scarlet embellished service dress. The rifle sling passes around the wearer's body, as was the Regimental practice at the time. In the horse kit, a white headrope and wallets over the front arch are used. Note the cloak strapped behind the saddle. *Author's collection*

Fig. 49: O.Rs' Full Dress Tunic *c.* 1903-1914, rear detail. White cord ornamentation as worn below staff serjeant. *Regimental collection*

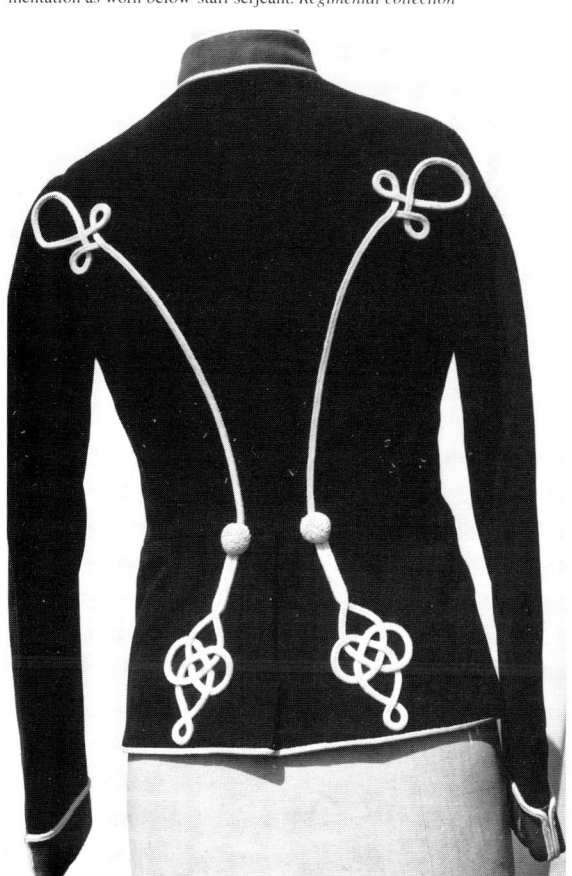

Fig. 48: (above) Front detail, O.R's Full Dress Tunic, *c.* 1903-1914. The O.Rs' pattern of braiding was universal, except that staff serjeants and above had all braid in silver. There are silver half-ball regimental buttons down the front. The silver lace chevrons are on scarlet backing, as is the gold and crimson crown. The rear detail is the same as in Fig. 49. This item was worn by S.S.M. Manley. *Regimental collection*

Fig. 50: Trumpeter, Full Dress, *c.* 1907-1908. This trumpeter shows clearly the uncrowned cap badge and the *c.* 1903, or last, pattern full dress tunic. The trumpet cords are of mixed blue, yellow and red, as for a Royal Regiment. *Regimental collection*

doliers and swords'. 'In future, bandoliers will always be worn on all duties instead of black pouch belts.'

Subsequent entries from the Orderly Books inform us 'Church *Parade – Men* Swords for all who have been issued with them. Bandoliers will not be worn'. 17 May 1902, and on 19 May 1902 '*Main Guard* will parade with pantaloons, puttees, ankle boots and jack spurs, instead of overalls and Wellington boots. Slings will always be carried with rifles, being attached to the lower band and butt swivel.' In 1906, a new forage cap was issued to the men. It was of the peaked staff pattern which had been worn by the officers from 1903 and was blue, with scarlet band and piping.

Effectively, from 1906-07, undress as such ceased to exist officially for the men. However, in the period 1908-1914, the ORs were allowed to purchase at their own expense plain all blue serge frocks with shoulder chains bearing insignia. There were five buttons down the front, pleated or unpleated breast patch pockets and, in some cases, patch pockets below the waist, with or without

Fig. 51: Lieutenant Colonel A. H. Heath and the Officers, Trentham Park Camp, 1907. With the exception of the Inspecting Officer, who is in blue undress (seated fourth from right) and an officer from the Lincolnshire I.Y. (extreme right, standing) all the officers wear khaki service dress. The Adjutant, Captain Jameson, 14th Hussars, wears a plain khaki cap (seated, third from left). *Collection of N. Mander*

Fig. 52: Lieutenant Colonel W. Bromley-Davenport, D.S.O., *c.* 1907-8. Note the pre-1900 braided frock coat, worn as an option by officers when off duty on Sports Days and Sundays in camp 1903-1914.
Author's collection

Fig. 53. Lieutenant Colonel C. T. Mander, 1909. Lieutenant Colonel Mander wears the officers' pattern khaki serge frock as worn between *c.* 1904 and 1913-14. Note the khaki cover to the top of Colonel Mander's blue and scarlet 'dress' forage cap. *Collection of N. Mander*

Fig. 54: The Machine Gun Section, 1910. While the officer on the left of the picture scans the distance, the men attend to some problem with the gun. Two of the team are clearly still wearing the first pattern, scarlet embellished khaki frocks and the scarlet piping is visible on the pantaloons of the man at the extreme right. *Regimental collection*

Fig. 55: Group of Officers on Church Parade, Croxton Park Camp, 1910. The officers in this group wear the smart Parade Dress with full dress silver laced pouch belts and sword slings, while the men in the distance wear forage caps with full dress tunics and overalls. *Regimental collection*

pleats; there were buttons throughout on the breast pocket flaps and, if present, on those below the waist. As these garments were paid for by the men a great deal of latitude seems to have been allowed. This last, unofficial undress uniform may be seen in Fig.61. As will be noted, the dress peaked forage cap, overalls, Wellington boots and white gloves completed this kit, which was confined to off duty and social wear about camp.

Fig. 56: Lieutenant Colonel W. Bromley-Davenport, D.S.O., T.D., and the Officers, *c*. 1911. Undress uniform is worn throughout and all have white cap covers and plain blue trousers. The Orderly Officer is distinguished by a pouch belt and the Adjutant, Captain H. B. Towse, Royal Scots Greys (seated, third from left) by his white vandyked cap hand. Another Royal Scots Greys officer is also present, seated first right. *Collection of N. Mander*

Officers Mess Dress

Officers continued to wear the stable mess jacket which has been described under 'Uniform 1881-1893' (Fig.25) up to, and after, 1900. However, Regimental Orders of 24 February 1894 inform us that officers stable jackets had undergone some slight alterations. The back and hind arm seams were now piped with scarlet cloth, Lancer fashion. Mess waistcoats were to have only lace edging and facing lace around the pockets. The fronts were otherwise to be plain. Further particulars are to be gleaned from tailors' notes of the late 1890s, which describe the mess and stable jacket as blue, lined with scarlet silk; scarlet collar and cuffs; scarlet piping up the back and down the hind arm seams. The lace is described as straight round the cuff (refers to rear of cuff) and of silver Artillery pattern with a scalloped edge, 1¼in wide for field officers and ⅜in wide for other officers. This refers to the lace edging the collar, all round the garment's edges and over the cuffs. Not listed in these tailors' notes are the following features to be seen on surviving garments: silver chain gimp around the base of the collar; shoulder cords, also of chain gimp with a small silver button and gold embroidered badges of rank; two small silver buttons over the cuffs at the hind seam; a row of tiny seed studs down the left front edge of the jacket. Overalls with footstraps were the prescribed full dress items, with double ¼in diamond centre silver lace side stripes, worn over Wellington boots with fixed dress spurs. From directions to be found in a memo to regimental tailors date 13 February 1903, it would appear that the Regiment was already taking steps to bring the uniform into line with the new regulations. With regard to officers' mess kit, it states 'Old kit to be worn out, overalls with either silver or cloth stripes; if new kit is required the new regulation jacket (with) scarlet silk roll collar and silver badges; scarlet cloth shoulder straps; scarlet cuffs with 1in slit (at rear edge); scarlet waistcoat (cut low, with four small buttons; overalls with scarlet stripes.' Completing the kit was a white shirt and collar with a black bow tie.

Fig. 58: Major G. P. Heywood, September 1911. The full Dismounted Review Order is worn by Major Heywood, who is shown as he appeared when, as a captain, he commanded the Staffordshire detachment at the Coronation in June 1911. *Regimental collection*

Fig. 57: Guard of Honour at the Opening of the new Drill Hall at Wolverhampton, 1911. Here only the officers wear busbies and it is interesting to note from the back view of the officer in the centre of the picture that the handsome old pattern pouch is still in use. It will also be noted that the serjeant on the left carries a sword. *Regimental collection*

Fig. 59: Lieutenant C. A. Mander and his No. 1 Troop, 'D' Squadron, Winners of the Regimental Cup, 1912. Plain regulation service dress is worn throughout and the bandoliers are of the 1903 leather, 50 round, 5 compartment pattern issued from 1909. *Author's collection*

Fig. 60: Private, Mounted Drill Order, *c.* 1913. Regulation plain khaki service dress is worn. The short Lee Enfield rifle is now carried high, with the sling short and over the arm, not, as earlier, around the body. The saddle is stripped and a white headrope is used. *Author's collection*

Field or Service Dress 1901-1903
Probably the first item of more practical kit to be adopted in the wake of the Boer War was a slouch hat (Fig.38) which was very similar to those worn in the South African campaign. Introduced for all ranks at Home in 1901, they were of drab felt, with a pagri or turban of about six folds of drab cloth around the body of the hat. The brim, which was bound at the edge, was turned up on the left side and bore a metal badge in the form of a simple Stafford Knot, mounted on scarlet cloth which showed through the loops of the knot. A narrow leather chin strap completed the headgear. There is no evidence of a plume ever being worn with this headdress during its short service up to 1903. It was thereafter discontinued, but is to be seen in photographs being worn by the men for fatigues or off duty in camp.

Khaki uniform for the Home Service Staffordshire Yeomanry is not thought to have appeared generally before 1904. The first mention of it appears to be found in the Regimental Orderly Books for January 1903 when reference is made to 'Khaki pantaloons and ankle boots with spurs for recruits', and an entry later the same year reads 'slouch hats will only be worn when expressly ordered'. Again, while referring to drill order for camp in 1903, it states that 'the forage cap (pill box), or service cap (field) if not in possession of a forage cap' would be worn. The same applied to blue or khaki serge jackets, blue or khaki pantaloons and blue or khaki puttees. All of the above leads to the conclusion that, although a change was being considered and certain steps were taken during the years 1901-1903, the uniform of the Staffordshire I.Y. worn for drill or field dress was, in fact, a combination of either the slouch hat or forage cap and a variety of the old blue serge undress and a few new items of uniform and new accoutrements. Surprisingly, for a period when photographic evidence is generally abundant, very little relating to this unit can be traced for the years 1901-1903. However, from the one or two photographs available it has been possible to confirm most of the points in the Regimental Orderly Books and tailors' memos. The following details of an important photograph in the Regimental Collection which showed a parade in mounted drill order about 1901 or 1902 were recorded some years ago. All ranks wore slouch hats but the badges were not visible; all wore blue serge frock but only officers and senior NCOs had shoulder chains, the remainder having blue cloth shoulder straps with titles; all wore blue riding pants with double scarlet stripes. Sam Browne belts were worn by the officers, who carried swords, and web bandoliers and rifles by the men. Another photograph of this period, in this case published in the *Navy and Army Illustrated* in July 1902 shows 2nd Lieutenant B. Hardy of the Staffordshires among a group of officers from other yeomanry corps attending the Imperial Yeomanry School at Aldershot. Lieutenant Hardy wears the slouch hat and blue serge frock, as worn in the mounted parade photograph, but without the Sam Browne belt. Lastly, another photograph taken at the School in the previous year (1901) shows three Staffordshire officers dressed in blue serges, but here wear-

Fig. 61: Group of Other Ranks, 1913-1914. Full Dress and Undress. Note the encrowned cap badges. *Author's collection*

ing scarlet field service caps piped silver (as Fig.37); one officer clearly wears blue pantaloons and puttees with ankle boots. Documentary evidence in the form of a regimental memo for the benefit of military tailors provides further confirmation of uniforms at this time. It clearly states (February 1903) that officers' service dress consisted of 'Blue serge, brown gloves, pantaloons either blue or brown (actually drab), Sam Browne belt, brown leather scabbard and sword knot, black field boots (knee boots) or blue puttees and black laced ankle boots and spurs, felt hat (slouch hat), red forage cap (pill box cap) as before. New cap to be settled later on and will replace the red forage cap'. It was further ordered that officers discontinue use of the scarlet field service cap.

Khaki Service Dress 1904-1914
As previously stated, khaki service dress is thought first to have been generally worn at the annual training of 1904. The officers' uniform consisted of the newly introduced blue and scarlet peaked staff pattern forage cap (Fig.45) as described in 'Undress 1894-1914'. Although this cap continued to be worn with the khaki service dress for some years, by about 1911 it is thought to have been replaced by the plain khaki cap for service wear. A khaki mixture serge frock was worn. It had a plain stand and fall collar, two patch and pleated breast pockets with pointed flaps and a button and two large expanding plain patch pockets which had straight cut flaps and buttons below the waist. There were five buttons to fasten down the front and the narrow shoulder cords each had a small button at the top. The shoulder cords, regulation rank badges and prescribed braiding on the sleeves were all in khaki mixture worsted (Figs. 51 and 53). Darkish shade plain Bedford cord riding pantaloons which were laced at the knees were worn with tan leather knee or field boots with jack spurs, leather straps and shields. The universal Sam Browne belt with sword in brown leather scabbard and tan leather wrist gloves completed the kit. Blue cavalry cloaks continued in service for some years after the introduction of khaki. Photographs taken about 1908 show that the officers chargers still carried white horsehair throat plumes and that white headropes were used. Brief tailors notes dated 20 March 1913 inform us that, by this date at least, the officers' khaki service jackets had acquired open cut collars, which were ordered for wear with 'khaki War Office flannel shirts and polo collars of starched double Oxford style'. Also listed were 'drab silk poplin ties'.

For the other ranks, the new service dress comprised the old pattern, pre-1900 scarlet pill box, still braided according to rank for the NCOs which have been described under 'Uniform 1881-1893'. The khaki mixture serge frock worn by the men was distinguished by having a scarlet stand collar and scarlet cloth shoulder straps with buttons and insignia as in Figs. 46-47. There was scarlet braid edging

Fig. 62: Church Parade, Patshull Camp, 1914. *Author's collection*

the khaki cuffs, which formed a trefoil over the point. Five buttons fastened the front of the coat and there were two plain breast patch pockets with pointed flaps and buttons. The NCOs' rank chevrons appear from photographs to have been of silver lace, or, less likely, exceptionally light shade drab. The drab cord riding pantaloons of darkish shade featured narrow scarlet piping in the side seams and were worn with khaki puttees, ankle boots and jack spurs with straps. Web single round cartridge bandoliers were carried up to 1909, when they were replaced by the regular 1903 pattern leather, five compartment fifty round type. At the same time, the short S.M.L.E. rifle replaced the earlier pattern. When the blue and scarlet peaked 'dress' forage cap was issued to the men in 1906 it was, at first, worn with the service dress (Fig.47) but was fairly quickly reserved for wear with full dress, and a plain regular pattern khaki cap was introduced for service dress about 1909. Likewise, the distinctive scarlet embellished khaki serge jackets were gradually phased out from about 1909 and plain regular khaki frocks were served out (Figs.59-60). The scarlet piped pantaloons persisted for some years before finally being replaced by plain items. Khaki greatcoats replaced the old blue cloaks.

It is interesting to note that, prior to about 1909, although the men carried the rifle in the customary short butt buckets on the off side, it appears from photographs that it was not the practice to carry the sling either over the right shoulder or elbow (Fig.60). The long sling went over the wearer's left shoulder and around his body, drawing the rifle across the back of the yeoman. This was not unheard of, but was not widely done in the Force.

Sources

P.G.G. Webster, *The Records of the Queen's Own Royal Regiment of Staffordshire Yeomanry*, 1870.

Regimental Orderly Books and other records held by the Staffordshire County Record Office in Stafford.

The collections of the Army Museums Ogilby Trust; R.J. Marrion; K. Hook; and the authors.

F.J. Johnson, M.A., Ed., *Victorian Cheadle, 1841 to 1881*, 1991.

Benson F.M. Freeman, R.N., *Historical Records of the Queen's Own Royal Staffordshire Imperial Yeomanry*, 1907.

Manuscript volumes by P.W. Reynolds in the Victoria and Albert Museum's collection.

Navy and Army Illustrated.

The Regiment.

Tailors notes